VARIATIONS

By

Jaroslav HAVELKA

P.S.A. VENTURES

London, Canada

Other books by P.S.A. Ventures:

THOUGHTS On Relationships by Paul Liebau

THOUGHTS On The Self by Paul Liebau

THOUGHTS On Purpose by Paul Liebau

THOUGHTS On Living by Paul Liebau

Copies available at your bookstore
or contact the publisher:

P.S.A. Ventures
80 Empire Street
London, Ontario
Canada N5Y 1G7

Published October 1988

Canadian Cataloguing in Publication Data

Havelka, Jaroslav, 1922
    Variations

ISBN 0-9691999-5-3

1. Aphorisms and apothegems. I. Title.

PN6271.H38 1988   C818'.5402   C88-095060-9

Printed in Canada

ACKNOWLEDGEMENTS:

I would like to thank to the following very deeply for their inspiration, encouragement and participation:

Pamela Fellows, for her faith in this work, her insightful understanding and warm criticism

John Orange, for his superb editorial skills, his literary advice and his patience with my stubborn idiomatic dilemmas

Ian Hunter, for his friendly willingness to read and critically evaluate, both astutely and kindly, and for his encouragement

Paul Liebau, for his sensitive and generous help with the publication

Imants Baruss, and Ted Osborne for their kind assistance in programming and laser printing

Lea Nevett, for her skillful and dedicated help in the final proof-reading

If the heart could grasp the meaning of life, in death it would know the mystery of God; Today when you are in possession of yourself, you know nothing. Tomorrow when you leave yourself behind, what will you know?

Omar KHAYYAM

Had I be present at the Creation, I would have given some useful hints for the better ordering of the universe

Alphonso the Wise

Our life is a complex variation on a theme: 'Who are you', 'Who am I', and what is reality. Our personal existence is a shifting but often sharp dividing line between the internal 'me' and the external 'not-me'. This socially induced dualism generates most of our conflicts and anxieties. Only in genuine human maturation is there a shift toward wholeness, where the boundaries between inside and outside diminish and disappear. Let us consider some of the variations...

$$\Omega$$

Even when I was an unshaven greenhorn I longed for something unknown. In women, in men, and in simple things. Today I long for it as well but somewhat less eagerly when, with a bowed head, I walk through the never-aging grass, so gently swaying in one direction. As it keeps pointing, I am more assured

$$\Omega$$

Do I miss the essentials in my life? I may not. As long as I remain the unfinished and fermenting dough of a loaf of bread

Ω

Mind thinks and argues with the world. Soul meditates on, and cherishes the world. Somewhere there exists a meeting point at which we mature by way of understanding

Ω

Although not yet in the main stream of life's present actuality we are always creation's promise. We already firmly endure while not yet born -- and our death cannot do anything about it. Death can never endanger a promise made by creation

Ω

When a dog yawns, it's time to feed him or take him for a walk; when a bridge player yawns, you have obviously a better hand; when a politician yawns, you have exhausted your usefulness to him; when a saint yawns, his God has missed a scheduled air-flight; when God yawns, it's time for a new Big Bang

Ω

Individual life is suffering. The life of each of us: separate, unrelated, unhealthily self-protruding, self-contracted, foolishly waiting for its own salvation, a jealous life of self-preoccupation, life programmed to be more effective in hoarding and boasting. This life, we know so well, is suffering. But life, universal life, is not suffering, just as the immense sky is beyond the temporary turbulance of the clouds. Life is self-inhering and exempted from any tragedy, pathology or sinfulness. Individual life is uncertain, staggering, limping, while universal life is rhythmical and immensely coordinated. Individual life creates evil; life is innocent. We are sad, hostile and sanctimonious. Life is wonder, delight and hilarity. Life and the reality of God is undivided. We, in our individual lives,either conceive God through suffering or arrogantly and unhappily proclaim His non-existence. Thus our theodicy is sad as is our dying. Life doesn't include death as any singularity but as a natural process of transformation

Ω

We often talk to prevent our mind from sinking through a hole of anguish. We imagine that talking is an escape: yet it is only a regression into the darkness of unknowing

Ω

Any sentence about death is essentially empty and false because it points at something which, not being there, is irrelevant in itself. Any sentence about dying is real because it points at reality,just as the dry branch of a pine-tree points at a space between our frightened eyes

Ω

Sometimes I fear joy as a mother fears her unborn child who speaks in an unknown language in the dark cathedral of her body. Sometimes I fear joy since I expect sorrow to be born

Ω

3

Deep joy is, surprisingly, a thought on the first post-mortem breakfast. It is a golden hook on which to hang the heavy bag of our tribulations.   Deep joy is a growing mushroom that pushes up an insignificant piece of earth on its humble hat -- winning against the mighty power of gravity

Ω

Bright brains are not bright because they grasp faster and more, but because they grasp the essential. They don't know more, but they have a deeper understanding.   I wish our universities educated bright brains and not clever and shrewd brains

Ω

The month of November impresses me. It empties the country-side, simplifies the curvature of branches, and stills the smallest capillaries of growth. It introduces the gardens to the cemeteries and,with a sigh of longing for the distant stars and through cold and silent rain, enters the graves of the chronic sleepers of eternity

Ω

Moses sat in front of a burning bush transfixed and immobile. He surely didn't want to call a fire-brigade to extinguish the fire that could threaten the villas of rich Pharisees. Social responsibility has its busy strategies; spirituality has none

Ω

I find myself at the end of a golden afternoon, when the approaching evening is punctuated by a radiant dust of insects,accompanying my dreams of the past. I imagine that I am walking memories of my closest friends on a leash like a faithful dog. As in the words of an old song, my friends loom high on the other side of the brook of passing time. They are the reliable ancient ones. I have cut out of the yellowing imaginary album, pictures showing their heads and shoulders, and now I glue them carefully onto the other side of the treasure-chest of my longing.

A warm tiredness stays with us as we walk to the promised land of our final reunion. We all walk this long journey where a benign mist passes through the window of our long lost childhood. A mist passes by allowing the ever amazing stars to send a distant gleam to the foreheads of all those memorable ones that mark my slightly nostalgic heart. Even when not too much remains in the cupboard of life's generosity, the honey of their friendship tastes so sweetly. I am so grateful that they have been, and that they keep blending with me.

Often, almost inadvertently, I turn back from the darkening frame of a window through which I see them passing. Then there is the last short gesture of my hand to confirm their goodness, which when lodged in the crystal of the past, always gently hurts. There remains the imaginary picture of us three musketeers with blissfully silly smiles, left a long time ago somewhere behind the receding Pleiades as a simple reminder of human reality. Somewhere all of them are guarding, as I do, a treasure beyond gold's value, and we keep singing the windy cantata of our careless youth.

I know that all human friendship is a breath on glass that rapidly evaporates -- yet it leaves behind indelible fingerprints of those who touched our hearts by breathing on them

Ω

Some of us know very little. Some of us know nothing. Yet some of us chisel futile sentences in spite of everything

Ω

The fact that I have slept one third of my life fills me with deep bewilderment.   Is my sleep a very expensive repair shop for my existence?   Do I then pay too high a tax for my survival or shouldn't I be rather grateful that for one third of my life I remain in close contact with the mysterious roots of universal consciousness -- which transcends my ordinary wakeful consciousness?   Do I have reason to complain or to be grateful? Is that a proper question?

Ω

As crooked as the torn-off wing of a bird is the memory of an unhappy love

Ω

People are afraid of aloneness, my grandfather used to say, because to find that rare herb and to use it well requires courage. To see a rose when alone, to hear a robin when alone, to write to a friend when alone, to think of God when alone, all require courage since, in order to do such things one must face a burning bush of truth: to cherish oneself while longing for the other in detachment

Ω

An illuminated sentence is a high tone celebrating the maturing wheat of mystery

Ω

Most of our compassion is based on our emotional hunger. Our helping, serving, and our concern for others are only gestures toward compassion. Mainly it is a way of improving our suffering self-image through self-preoccupation and self-congratulation. As long as there is a distinction between the giver, the receiver, and the gift, compassion is incomplete because it is dualistic and self-directed. Real compassion is totally selfless, non-profitable, discrete and ever-present. It doesn't yearn for recognition and rewards. It is a loving-kindness for its own sake

Ω

There is nothing left even for God under an unlifted boulder. Nothing but a joy which counteracts any gravity

Ω

Diary writing is for conceited people as they daily boast about their self-importance, while their impertinent cuteness is an effort to paint over a looming insecurity. Diary writing is for wise people as they daily notice more and more their insignificance against the background of immensity. They use it more as good-hearted self-joking or as a cosmic sigh. The former diarists take a picture of the moon to display publicly their collection of photographs; the latter kind point their fingers to the moon and remain silence stricken . Now, which one are you?

Ω

Aloneness doesn't demand much. It is self-contained like the waters of a placid lake. It resembles a lighthouse overturned into a deep well where its revolving eye captures the sight of shimmering stars reflected there even at high noon

Ω

Consider that it is quite possible that the basic state of the human condition is happiness. If that is our base, it should follow that one cannot become happy but only re-enter the original state of happiness. Thus unhappiness is only a postponement of happiness and not a state of reversed polarity or the non-existence of happiness. Unhappiness is a process, not a state, during which we are obstructed from attaining the original state. Only happiness is our original state and unhappiness is an egotistic interference with it. Thus, again, we cannot become happy but we can only rediscover our original condition. There human spirituality begins

Ω

A joyous moment of freedom in universal destiny: a falling leaf as it leaves its place on the branch and before it touches the earth

Ω

Even the smallest event, gesture, feeling, joy, is a burning instance in the furnace of constant recasting. It is final, unrepeatable and impermanent. Even our death is unrepeatable and thus bound to recasting

Ω

Serenity is the privilege of hearing a sound evoked by the gentle jump of a sparrow accompanied by the sound of a falling leaf

Ω

There are abandoned shores where a wading bird drawn by the pen of loneliness punctuates the paper of a grey horizon. Beyond it only a dominion of melancholy

Ω

Our soul , similar to an atom, longs for fusion. An immense heat is necessary to achieve it. The more fractured we are, the more we long to cease to be fragments. In the arresting moment of love, a transforming flame poises like a royal cobra, signalling with its awesome eye that spot in us where it is about to strike and cause the split to heal

Ω

Only by a radical transformation of our life's staging will we attain higher maturation. Life without transformation is self-contracted misery and unhappiness. It is worthwhile, I guess, to be born just for that potential for transforming in each of us

Ω

A woman of false love cherishes in a man the immaculate image of herself which he carries in his heart -- and nothing else

Ω

Before being born we are like self-oblivious singing angels, who in the flared conflagration of the divine presence do not crack. Before the mysterious crack of being born as individuals, we are eternally conceived but not yet made, like Mozart's sonata in the first second of Creation. We do not want anything yet, be it a small puppy, a silvery dance-shoe, a woman's love, a new stereo set, a benign configuration of destiny, or even a blissful pain in our soul which signals our longing for God.   All that will come later, when the webb of hair-line cracks will appear in our lives as on the glaze of an ancient Chinese vase, signalling the advent of our self-awareness. All that will come much later, while our sorrow deepens and our fragmented lives seem beyond repair

Ω

The best moments of our lives should be like the burning top of a tree after a visitation of lightening, when all that is cheap, worrying, dishonest, cruel, sad and unsubstantial is consumed in the light of recognition

Ω

The wise ones consider bliss, as contrasted with joy, as a divine sieve which functions amazingly by letting everything pass, by not holding and grasping anything, and becoming an instrument of total freedom

Ω

Most of us are inflated balloons with a diminishing air-pressure. And our modern civilization is mostly a conveniently installed chain of air pumps. The slogan is: 'Keep the pressure up or bust'

Ω

Already in the early afternoon some of us long to go home while still listening to the silent reading of the Magna Carta of our life's enchantment. When the darkness falls, no more sound but only the lingering memory of our unforgettably loyal Mother of everything

Ω

The shape of human life is moulded by the expanding pressure of existence and by the gravitational pull of death. Our mist-shrouded intimation before being born goes eventually through the dynamic pressure chamber of our personal destiny -- before we rain out again into the great Void. We travel from a creative abstraction of our pre-origin to an inevitable abstraction of our post-mortem dispersal. The tragedy of our existence is that while God knows us as an enduring promise, we experience ourselves as failures

Ω

We church people resemble the ancient Russian bojars clad in the best bear furs, as we carry the ice-cube of our false belief into our chosen sanctuary. Our main task is to deliver to the high altar that awkward and dripping burden before it melts; before it melts as a result of our insecurity and the nervously hectic breathing of our suspicious devotion. Through sheer frustration we cross ourselves very often, so that this solemn gesture locks us into the frozen twist of a mummy. Meanwhile the ice-cube of our phony belief is rapidly melting and it drips from our trembling hands -- yet the Tzar, still so distant, still so many chambers away from us.

We know what we are longing for but because we long for it only for our own sake and for our own salvation, the ice-cube of our shabby belief becomes a pool of lukewarm water as useless to us as it is to a Tibetan swallow

Ω

11

cinema of my dreams? Maybe it is because in that mysterious lining of life's twilight I am reading a handwritten message in a language unknown to me, yet deeply trusted. Things appear in it both misty and sharp-focussed. Some sort of riddle is awaiting an unexpected deciphering and when that occurs, the dream is no more. Thus the dream is never too certain of itself; it is something that shyly disappears as soon as I know it is a dream.

Dreams pass by like meteorites that have just left the dark side of a distant planet. They orbit the simplest things, sometimes slightly out of focus, always pertinent and yet so remote. Like a skillful waiter serving us breakfast in the grass, while a snake hides in the innocent salad. A dream is the most exchangeable commodity for reality beyond our understanding. There is a duality to it, a confusing 'halo' effect. A dream always contains its contradiction, and thus whatever it portrays is dramatic.

Every dream seems to adhere to a dual reality: how to escape a gaping horror and how to remain in contact with a protective hand. Pungent smoke lifts from an endless procession of dreams, where a witche's brew is distilled into deadly poisons to make the inchoate language of myths miraculously precise. Most dreams have a tendency to go the way of death, making us progressively heavier without a will, and causing us to gravitate towards some absorptive centre, as death does.

When sometimes I dream of the famous of this world, they are usually playing together in a sand-box surrounded by a crowd of clowning banalities. And instead of being impressive and heroic, those famous ones weakly cry on my shoulder. Futhermore there is another problem in the dream: I never know who is the host and who the guest. Thus there follows a fascinating play of hide-and-seek where the role of the captive and the jailer are interchangeable.

At last I leave the cinema of my dreams where I see myself living on a huge screen. When the show is over I rush to an uncanny looking attendant and ask him again and again if I am going to a place where I have already been, or returning to somewhere I have never been.

Why am I often so uneasy about leaving my

12

dreams? Maybe it is because in that mysterious lining of life's twilight I hear an accusation spoken in a voice strangely familiar to me yet outside the reach of my memory

Ω

It doesn't really matter whether you wait for the Devil's landau to stop at the broken bridge of your life. Nobody steps out of it anyway -- just your ego and your own unhappiness

Ω

If we suffer from a cancer of sin, some uncanny intimations whisper behind the door of our ward, which, although unlocked, doesn't permit us to exit and to see ourselves as cured patients. An amputated sin still remains a part of the sinner's body

Ω

A communicator's nightmare: a row of insatiable vultures sits on a withered branch, agitated by a wind issued from timeless truth, and they watch us with malicious suspicion as we nervously struggle for expression

Ω

The autumn sun doesn't know what to gild first: the valley of my anxiety or the hill into which the mole of my hope burrows an underground map for homecoming

Ω

A culture that isn't based on the assumption of the transcendence of Being over individual existence is a pseudo-culture. It is exclusively ego-dominated, mechanical and surrounded by materialistic scientism. It tries to control and organize through instinctual motives, cheap sentimentality and hedonistic rationality. Such a pseudo-culture is extraordinarily banal as a large part of modern fine art and modern music is. It is usually a show-off not of radical simplicity but of instinctive primitivism that aims at gratifying the most immature, lustful, and mindlessly crude aspects of human desires. It is an attempt for trivial democratization, levelizing and agressive communization of the human condition.

This rampant psychic degeneration is at the centre of our modern civilization. It leads to a disastrous abdication of any spirituality since human spirituality is a realization of and gratitude for our inseparable tie with the universe. Without it we remain stuck with commercial advertising, muzak, girlie magazines, T.V. evangelism, international politics, and the constipated wish to become human beings while committed to a hominoid level of social mediocrity

Ω

It is sheer frustration to be polite all the time: to present ourselves to the world in black tie and always oblige to scrape the floor with our shoe, like a bitch after watering on a lamp-post, in a gesture of sanctimonious and phony deference. After all what do we think the others think they are?

Ω

Why not be like a simple chair in a splendid coronation hall? Nobody fusses about it, nobody pays attention. And the less noticed it is, the more it exists in the austere space of freedom, of non-attachment. Only its companion, an elongated shadow, projects its significance

Ω

14

We should be more aware that our waking experience is dreamlike. Although perhaps more rational and familiar, it is not more substantial than a dream. Accordingly, we no longer have to treat life as too serious a problem. After all, its essential character can be expressed in 'as if' -- not really different from dreaming. Thus only when we attempt to unify our waking state and our dream state, then may we reach a deeper reality. When we remove what separates day-dreaming from night-dreaming, real and un-real become one. Who knows -- maybe our whole existence is being dreamt. But the rub is, who is the dreamer?

Ω

Bitter is an after-life without God. Meanwhile, we wait for a crack in the crystal vase of despair through which grace may lighten the darkness of our grave. Bitter is an after-life without God. Then the grave remains dark even if a small hole left after the extracted flower allows a narrow beam of light to fall on the bent knees of the dead ones, endlessly dreaming about the bitterness that exists without God

Ω

On the wide wasteland of our dried-out lives endures dry grass whose sharp hiss is a commentary on our longing for Him, our most indispensible water-vendor

Ω

A Sunday morning for a devout peasant: a page from an old breviary on which an artless hand has drawn a simple steeple that runs past the margin of the page
Ω

How much have I explained to others without really understanding myself? I have failed because I have missed the most amazing significance of everything as it emerges from the darkness to become illuminated not for its purpose but for its meaning

Ω

When we die, no more this shabby bachelor's dish of the reheated maccaroni of futile emotions along with the bitter salad of troubling thoughts sprinkled with stupid seasoning. What a laugh to be at last on vacation with guaranteed room and board! How amusing to hear our beloved music permanently recorded in our amazed hearts. To meet again all our long-departed dogs and other friendly creatures, ghosts and apparitions. How exhilarating to know that there won't be any glittering heavenly reception, no waiting for His Majesty's audience, no angels singing the Messiah -- but just the opportunity to meet the immense, the invisible, the inscrutable, the hidden, the mysterious. To inhale the loveable, to exhale the compassionate, to laugh with a crazy, new geometry and at fresh Jewish jokes, and to sing in a sympathetic attunement with cosmic energy. I write this in a happy disposition, yet with some inexplicable nostalgia

Ω

I avoid dark thoughts as a half-broken fence avoids the cold autumn winds. Yet here it is again, the sonata of emptying and I am surrounded by it in a slow rhythm of unnecessary and yet so loyal tribulations

Ω

Vergil's death was neither sudden nor unexpected. He died as every real poet does: he entered the fissure between time and permanency as a guest for one night only. A guest who sleeps on an unopened travelbag with a flute in his teeth, ready to join the early tuning of the dawn. Some have insisted that he died of a sickness, others said that he died of his longing for Dante. His last letter was to Strabo with whom he shared his military tent during the siege of Vernum and to whom he dedicated the posthumous edition of his poetical work. His last will remained illegible, except for the five repeated words "...as if in a dream...". Some enthusiasts have tried to decipher other words but have always encountered a deep sound of warning that emanates from the unknown.

His last gesture was simple and unfinished: he shaved only half of his face and spilled the remaining soapy water out of the window on an adulating and noisy crowd. His last longing was to stand alone in the midst of crackling sheaves of wheat accompanied by a choir of crickets. His last memory was of a long-past morning, when out of the fog's gentle cotton slowly emerged a poplar tree which kept whispering ever so faintly something of great importance. When they carried out his body, like that of Hamlet's, a poplar's leaf aimed at a gaping hole and several times resisted earth's gravity.

Very little remains of a dead poet. Yet what remains endures in the motionless radiance of a human heart ready to reflect upon itself

Ω

Just imagine: when at last we enter the Divine hall, the walls may recede and emptiness may suddenly fill all Its immense reality. Then we may know a benediction that never ends. If all our personal existence were to aim at that -- how worth-while it would be to live

Ω

When we are most truthful to ourselves,we find that only then can we laugh uproariously. Only then can we appreciate any cosmic joke intimating that everything is safe, secure and good. That is the meaning of the Hindu's LILA

Ω

Blooper: Almost every time I open my mouth, some fool speaks. Corrected blooper: Almost every time I open my mouth, some fool interrupts me. After a moment's thought, blooper stands corrected but vindicated: Almost every time I open my mouth, some foolishness comes out

Ω

Belief and faith: what a deep difference. In our belief we are constantly demanding something, appealing to something or someone, invoking something or someone; we are proud of our belief like a seagull sitting on a mast in self-approval. We build churches out of this pride and install in them the central heating of sentimentality, instead of the church organ of faith. Through faith we may reach a state of non-agitated, benign and ego-less emptiness only after having first felt a sense of fullness. The resulting bliss doesn't come from obtaining something but from abandoning a great deal

Ω

Some great Russian said that nothing improves a man's character better than remembering his past with a contrite heart. He may be right, but then, building a character is an awfully painful undertaking

Ω

No doubt I took my life's curves too sharply and my travelbag has broken at the seams. Many things have been spilled and here I am rummaging among them: a photograph of my shy mother in a folk-costume, my father's watch that he carried through the war, my uncle's violin as he embraced it in a loving gesture of self-forgetting, my grandfather's walking stick with which he pointed which way the angels fly for an overnight rest among the stars. Many things have been spilled and now they are beyond recovery. But what if they reside somewhere else than in the memory of my unsteady brain? Is perhaps our memory preserved in some Universal Library of Congress to be attended by our Mothers, and thus never to be lost?

Ω

A fissure, a split, runs through me like a hair-line flaw passing through an ancient architrave. This split is in all of us, a sign of imperfection that happens in that decisive shift of energies when we are born. We are marked for individuality: we are cracked. I don't think animals have this original flaw. When born they don't crack into a restless self-reflection. They do not abandon themselves to a never-ending quest for certainty. Animals are probably unaware of their physical and psychic uniqueness; they peacefully ruminate on the timeless fringes of being. Their existence and its destiny doesn't worry them; their mere being is a sufficient guarantee of their unfragmented peacefulness

Ω

If our marriages are lived in the enjoyment of mutual dependency and satisfaction only, we are just fulfilling the ego's dominant desire. Our relational affection is self-gratifying and not linked to our basic condition of happiness; these affections, cutely called love, derive primarily from episodes of positive experiences which our egos propose to repeat in order to feel secure, self-satisfied and protected. If our marriages are lived as a vast programme of conventional self-approval and institutional prevention of loneliness, we have failed the test of maturity. We may resign ourselves to an obnoxious scenario of repeated upheavals and frustrations. We may lose the capacity to recover original happiness and thus become un-free. We may surrender to bondages, false expectations and patterns of reluctant and even unwanted cohabitation

Ω

Stupidity is endurable only through compassion. And if compassion goes beyond its limits, it has to be admired as a cardinal virtue. The unsettling fact is that stupidity never appreciates compassion's sisterly gesture, but merely begets new stupidity

Ω

If I trust you, I have freed you from any obligation. Your freedom is my reward and my security. If I don't trust you, I make rules, stipulate, state conditions. Your freedom is my frustration and my anger

Ω

Human stress is based on dependency --- a dependency, often obsessive, on things or relations that seem to enhance our egotism. The driving force of stress is a compulsion to seek something different, other, new, future. To seek arrangements and re-arrangements that will gratify our never satiated ego. We are driven to seek projected goals, escalated gratifications, simple or intricate strategies of success, prestige and approval. Stress appears to be our painful awareness that we have failed to succeed. Thus our hunger continues; the appliances are different, but the voltage is the same. Our stress, accompanying unfulfilled expectations, means that we seek consolation, comfort, distraction and release from the unhappiness of failure. Where is it more apparent than in our attachment to, and our preoccupation with, sex? Being almost permanently under stress, we realize the powerful urgency of release that sex offers. We continue to depend on it and are super-interested in it. Sex becomes an obssession, and without love it becomes a degenerative release disregarding the involved person yet dependent on the body target. Obviously, sex without love becomes the epitome of an explicitly self-gratifying and mutually exploitative act, often parading as caring and love. And so it often continues in our marriages. Even if it starts in a potentially genuine relationship, it reverts to a dependency bondage of interests and sexual gratifications. The dependency originates stress; sex becomes a relief-act and the social ritual of the owner and the owned is both vicious and sanctioned. Marriage can become a respectability and responsability trap of untold reproductive miseries easily leading to deep disillusions and unhappiness

Ω

What is the best gift people can give to each other? Confirmation of their cosmic origin, admiration for their uniqueness, and removal of their anxieties

Ω

When you disappoint me, there is a little hemorrhage in my heart; when you disappoint me again, the heart stops bleeding but a scar remains. How scar-ridden must be hearts of people who trust only death

Ω

The future of our civilization is uncertain; either we shall grow stronger in our religiosity and weaken in our religions -- or our religions will totally dominate. Whichever the case, our human posterity will always be closer to the angels. Either to the fallen ones or to the real messengers of God

Ω

Reality is not necessarily an event, a form of something, or an objective appearance. While we recognize it as such on the base of common sense, we are still not in a position to detect it. We can talk about it but not of it. Reality in the highest sense, like things divine, doesn't consist of 'things' at all but is a tendency-displaying being. Thus God can be imagined as a probability of potentially inescapable Isness that when objectified ceases to be divine

The Isness of any given moment is a radical, unabstracted yet totally indescribable Reality. Divine Reality is 'hidden' in every other sense than that It Is. God has not to be found as a specimen or object, as an emotion or a ghost behind the altar, but only experienced as Reality that Is. Any other attribute is explicit, derived from common rational sense and not inhering into the implicit order of Being. Love is an implicit order of Being, explicitly lived by us but irrevocably bound to the Reality of God. That is love's only Reality. Any other attribute, form or expression of love is often self-contracting -- and sentimental Narcissus

Ω

Often we pass each other like messengers in a Greek play, our faces dark with foreboding, and our body-space contracted and distorted. We hate this mindless and soul-less encounter but blame others. We have reached a level of dire disinterestedness and resentment and our intentions are both murderous and suicidal. We become depersonalized shadows chasing our own appearance. We have subtracted our humanity and cynically heap invectives upon it. We become acid rain falling on the ark of human hopes. We become malediction contradicting the benediction of our fundamental condition. We fear to be miscreants of creation as we pass each other in ever-widening orbits of light-years' distance

Ω

This morning I decided to walk on a mountain, an ancient harvest of boulders and pine trees. Everything had a peculiar circularity: the balloons of clouds, the stones and boulders, the round waves of a brook, the bushes of blackberries, and my joy of life. When one walks on a mountain, all things appear progressively more isolated and significant. Down in the valley, things are heaped in confusion, they are too many for one's attention. But on the first cliffs, things step out suddenly, meet your vision more than your sight, and the silence frames all, even your aloneness. Things stick out, protrude sharply, and a distant longing begins its flute sonata.

I was on my way to visit a mountain recluse. He has lived here for many years in some hidden caves and cliffs. Nobody asked where he belongs since for a long time he hasn't belonged anywhere. He welcomed me with open arms, in each hand a blue flower. On his face he had the smile of a cherub on vacation. He spoke to me with such a gentleness as if transferring cobwebs from a jasmin branch on the palm of his kindness. He was surrounded by a mist of absentmindedness, and when I was about to say something, he gently covered my mouth. Yet I still wanted to ask him something, I don't know what, but he wasn't there anymore. At a distant steep peak I saw a moving dot jumping from boulder to boulder like a spark from a flint

Ω

23

When people close to us are involved in dangerous situations, we worry. The moment they are safe, we are both relieved and annoyed. By being safe they have somehow lost part of their preciousness. In some strange way we are angry with them because they have spoiled our chance for self-gratifying sympathy.

Thus, our sympathy being needed no longer, we feel somewhat self-righteously deprived. In similar way, a worried love is usually preferred to a serene one. Yet, paradoxically, unworried love is greater because it has less self-pity, less self-righteousness and more detachment. Most of our cultures, however, consider an unworried love as not being worth a candle. Even great Shakespeare can make such a mistake

Ω

In our attempt to penetrate the silence -- we often fall asleep

Ω

Our heart can be as heavy as a stone dropped into a deep lake. For a short while there are some agitated waves and then silence. Life has swallowed our heaviness without a trace. Nobody knows it any more once it has buried itself in the dark bottom. The lake becomes serene again and life has returned to its detached equillibrium. Just some very distant stars blink as if in compassion

Ω

As a very little boy I cut out of paper my own drawing of a bird. It was my first 'creative' act. This bird must have been of a higher order of reality since when my mother inadvertendly swept it away, I howled with the pain of losing

24

something very precious. Where had I seen it first? Was I bemoaning Lost Paradise?

Ω

When our heart speaks, we are both happier and sadder. Happier because we are closer home and sadder because we have to leave again

Ω

I am not going to love you but I promise to be in love with the idea of loving you

Ω

When I walk the city streets that remind me of happier times, I feel sadder. Why don't I feel happy? Because the ego of today envies the ego of yesterday. We are our own enemies in more ways than one

Ω

Kindly listen to an old story of love: the story of Eloise and Abelard. How impatiently she used to wait for his ascent to the pulpit when she was a young Eloise and he a priest Abelard. He had a beautiful Augustinian beard, bristled with an aggressive innocence like an exposed electric wire, while she swooned in the radiant sweetness that surrounded the burning tissue of her inflamed heart.

Now, many years later, she is lonely and alone; lonely like the evaporated fragrance of incense. Abandoned, she contemplates his rotting remnants in glass reliquary, where she sees just a yellow cheek-bone tied to a jaw by an invisible band of sorrow. The sanctuary without her beloved Abelard is the den of church mice and of spiders who weave subtle strings that cannot sustain even the fallings of emaciated love. She stares, after a melancholy Mass, into a vault of void that arches over a perpetually painful shimmer of Abelard's image in the high, dark corners. She is a contorted statue in the darkening arch, one which sightlessly looks through a dusty window into the rapidly running rivulet of rain. She is a dead echo of two loves following each other in the church nave, like two solitary birds starving for light. Soon she will leave the church and moving through the rain like a shadow without an object

Ω

People leave each other thinking that living together makes them unhappy. But what if people are already unhappy and living together only confirms their ongoing unhappiness?

Ω

Every child knows that a cloudless sky is a round mountain. When adults have lost that image it changes into one of an awesome ever-receding void. Even a vague comprehension of immensity is chilling -- as every maturing is

Ω

When we drop something we say 'damn it!' -- yet that object follows the most elementary and life-preserving force, gravity. If the same object were to fly upward, we would undoubtedly say 'look at it!' wondering about its unusual behaviour. Our natural tendency toward perversion is basically a fear of boredom

Ω

The fantasy of a divine beach-comber, a saint: to lie down leisurely on his back and slowly to levitate toward God's radiance the way a drowned body is drawn from the bottom to the flowers of the waterlily

Ω

Why do most of us fail in our loving? Maybe we fail to understand what loving is and in so doing misundersand life itself. What about calling it our original sin? Anyway, it is half way to hell

Ω

If we lose an admission ticket to any joint or happening, we are barred from entrance as unworthy or illegal, and kicked out. Life is never so exclusive or cruel; it admits us freely and has only one warning -- not to sell ourselves too cheaply to our egos

Ω

Star-dust is continuously falling on us, star-dust which, in the day time, is like pollen from a golden flower, and during the night is like a silver mist. No wonder that we blink at the stars and the stars at us. Then we know that our eyes are the place of a wonderful encounter, a gentle touch of the immensity beyond us

Ω

Our ego-oriented belief is mostly thermotropic, a heat-seeking desire to be securely wrapped in, and protected from, the chills of our unhappy lives' winterstorms. It seems to be an insurance agent with a high deductible clause -- what it covers is always less than what it promises

Ω

27

Some of us enter the church, the ancient dominion of grace, and instead of falling to the marble floor in awe, we are attracted to the naive blue sky painted on the cracked ceiling, and greedily inhale a whiff of cheap consolation. For which of us, really, were built the churches, cathedrals, synagogues and mosques?

Ω

The pestilence of dehumanization dresses up our walking inflated corpses in gray flame. We learned doctors are at the end of our therapeutic wits, and no ecological alarm is being registered as we face the plentiful harvest of the bubonic plague of envy, violence and anxiety. A sweetish smell of decomposition reaches even the professional priests, ministers, and rabbis who take the pestilence as an affront to the reputation of their sterile belief. They can only offer their thin and mostly useless consolation like a plastic host that adheres annoyingly to the palate. Only reluctantly they admit that the ruptured bladder of pharisaic piety causes a galloping blood poisoning.

Only the spiritual ones among them speak the remaining language of liberating hope, but they are few and many miles apart, like registered nurses in Kenya. They join in trying to solve the insoluble cross-word puzzle of our destiny while knowing that our children face two awesome problems: how to survive, and, even more, how to survive uncontaminated

Ω

Do you remember ever seeing anything more self-admiring and self-important than a dashing flight-attendant in an airport terminal, or an intern in a hospital corridor, or a film 'star' at the Oscar ceremony, or a Professor reading a paper at a conference? One wonders whether the conceit is an understandible extravagance of mediocrity, or plain stupidity

Ω

The house is empty, or so it appears. All my feelings are attached to the absent dear people and animals aimlessly roaming with silent steps from room to room. Standing there I know that the life of feelings without their evokers is a theatre of shadows. The house is empty even with my feelings roaming from room to room

Ω

I am returning from a visit with my grandmother. Under my arm I was carrying a violin. I used to play for her after supper because she was still grieving for my deceased grandfather. The barking of the dogs closes over the evening village, like a squeaking gate, and the birds return from the projective geometry of a long day. The sky gapes empty like a motionless lake into which the reflection of a distant poplar has pierced a hole. The silence extends and at the end of its thin branch a bluejay gently swings, mindless of never-resting gravity.

She never knew what to say or what not to say, since both of these inclinations burned like a bare foot on a hot summer stone. As I leave, once more I look back swiftly to complete a postmortem mask of everything she saw only through my eyes, because, since his death she never stepped on the verandah of the house. I walk along the cherry-tree alley backwards, somehow wanting to keep that white-painted old house in sight, to which I brought since my childhood everything my eyes, my ears, and my heart, could carry.

Suddenly I remember my tears; tears that belonged to her just as much as her fading wedding scarf and grandfather's old, handsomely carved tobacco box. I didn't know what every woman knows so strongly: that the gathering of the flowers of man's enchantment precedes the noble art of making a bouquet of unforgettable love. Such a bouquet is God's decision to allow human hearts to retreat from the flame of awesome mystery to an ordinary life through the rainbow of happiness. I didn't yet know that behind that white-painted house the purest womanhood was sinking into abyss of loneliness where an immense conflagration singes her beloved's face into a contorted mask of sorrowful separation.

    I saw my grandmother peeled away from life like the aging bark from an oak tree. From her I have learned to fathom the summit of grief from which light falls to darkness, the other side of love. That darkness keeps falling on a mound of earth over which stumble the muddied hooves of little sheep -- memories driven by a relentless wind past grandfather's lonely house in the valley of twilight dreams with the distant echo of an unforgettable voice.

    The barking of the dogs closes over the evening village and not far away two lilac bushes whisper to a forest meadow that sheer womanhood and love are inseparable. I return from my grandmother, the violin under my arm, and in each closed fist and under my tongue lies a coin of pure compassion as payment for ferrying across the cold river of life

Ω

    The dark wood of the pews used to remind me of a quiet convoy of coffins that float on the wave of incense that never leaves the conclave of the church. Only the dead ones do

Ω

    The most delightful pranksters of the universe: a flock of omnipresent angels vigorously pulling along the church-nave the gilded wires of the telephone-line to the Supernatural

Ω

    For a million years the humble bumblebee still wrestles with flowers that close at dusk, like ancient Jacob with the angel. Why am I in such a hurry?

Ω

30

Young owls are voracious eaters who swallow avidly but fail to digest. We are all young owls to entertainment and diversions -- and not even the miracle of Pepto-Bismol will correct our indigestion

Ω

Some of my recurrent dreams have a common element: strange, uncanny Petrushka-like clowns, dressed half in gold and half in purple are mockingly obstructing my way; the ancient church-steeple seems to be progressively inclining; the sun stands in the zenith pensively staring at the huge canyon of a modern city. Someone I know is hardening into a salt-column in a street that ends at a wall with a freshly painted fresco of somebody's crucifixion

Ω

There is always someone, somewhere, who cries in his anxious dream, someone who mumbles incoherently about hidden beauties, someone just removed from a cross, and someone who has vertigo seeing the solitary rib of an unfinished cathedral

Ω

Sleeping children are still visited by a gentle touch of the boundless unknowing; they don't mind yet the looming holes in the socks of their future destiny, trusting that the angels are the best sock-menders of the universe

Ω

Most artists are amazed at the link between
seeing and suffering. Being creative they aim to transform both

Ω

A snapshot of modern cruelty: in the middle of
the street someone is burning a rose soaked in gasoline under a
pale, ironical, neon lamp

Ω

Predestination of our salvation smacks of
favouritism, thus smacks of an undemocratic breach of human
rights, and civil liberties defenders should be theologically
disgusted. And yet we should know that Calvin meant well

Ω

We know that a tree has undisturbed dreams,
even if a suicidal man sits under it. It was shortly before daybreak
when I saw him sitting under an oak tree. We were both returning
from a village dance. Around us the night was so full of
impressions that it was breaking at its seams in the distant horizon.
He was crying, his hands over his face, and the
erupting sobs were not coming from his throat but from some
hidden caverns of grief.   He was swaying and bowing to the oak
tree just as a faithful Jew does facing the Wall of Lamentations.
He spoke the unknown, desperate language of an injured soul.
Here and there: 'Jesus on the cross...' came from some distant
region of his childhood, from a dried-out territory before the
execution place of his love, from the awesome outreach of his
own crucifixion -- and yet the all-compassioned Mary did not rend

the sky to hasten to his help. Just the oak tree whispered some silent promise, forming the sad line of God's lips.

I didn't have anything particular to do and so the easiest thing would have been to take him in my arms. But I didn't. He was surrounded by an unearthly tempest of horrors that formed waves and eddies outside of the reach of any grace. Thus I couldn't reach him. At that time he was running against the sharp sword of his terrifying destiny over a ground covered by the rusty nails of his lost hopes. Now, he was no longer under the oak tree; now he was even beyond the forest and he may not have heard the warning whistle of an approaching train.

The oak tree was left leafing through its crown and was silent without a promise

Ω

When society dry-cleans our last shirt and hangs it on a clothes-line of rejection, some of us join it to hang ourselves. How far are we from the time when as unborn infants we were trustingly hanging on mother's cords within her loving body

Ω

A reason for Homeric laughter: to find on our car a ticket for illegal parking when on return from visiting a Gothic cathedral

Ω

Something beyond the pull of gravity urges me to kneel down. Reluctantly I crush the apples of my knees into sour wine and lean on God as on a rust-eroded railing through which whistles the futile wind of my bitter reason of little faith

Ω

Master looking at his dog: ' by now, he should understand some of my language'. Dog looking at his master: ' by now, he should understand some of my language'. God looking at both of them: "I am glad that they don't speak the same language. By now, their great friendship would have been finished"

Ω

Why do we clap after seeing or hearing something that is expected to be appreciated? Probably we want to be publicly noticed as appreciative, as having cultured understanding and good taste. No doubt, however, that this public demonstration of having 'class' outweighs the enjoyment of the performance itself. Let us be frank: after all, the sound of clapping is thoroughly barbaric -- especially after hearing a fine piece of music or an impressive theatrical performance. We erupt into disproportioned, non-melodious, odious noise without any form, and loudly -- the louder the better.

Do we want completely to destroy the effects of musical or theatrical reverberation in its profoundly significant fading away into silence? Or when an eloquent speaker leads us through the beautiful intricacy of logic or imagination -- must we throw in a hand-grenade of our banality and so contrast his civilized effort with our condescending, chaotic, tasteless and crude bombast? And the peak of banality is still to come: that is the 'quasi' enthusiastic explosion of the infamous ' Bravo!' or 'Brava!'. What do the screamers want to say!? That they just woke-up and are noisy through embarrassment, or that an Italian singer must be good and they have noticed that and show us their sophistication using the proper jargon.

And please notice that the timing of the explosion is aimed at a split second after he/she has finished singing and a split second before another enthusiast has a chance to flood us with a brutally throaty accolade. By the way, the audience of the Greek drama of the classical period followed the performance with rapt attention and yet never used this banality of ours. Is there any remedy for this atrocity? None.

Ω

When a huge mountain shadow falls on a field of dandelions, no harm is done. An enormous gentleness descends on an exquisite subtlety. A ready-made metaphor for loving-kindness

Ω

In a festive mood, when in friendship with the world, I follow the clouds, these orphans from nowhere to nowhere, to circumnavigate Haydn's 'Creation'. And I imagine with joy in my heart, that I was born mainly so that someone would compose an Oratorio on my behalf

Ω

Some people enjoy being in jail not for being in jail, but for anticipating the future release

Ω

Heather smells strongly in the silent gliding of another evening, and promises to stay together with a rustling breath over the silent arm of the river. Something ever-so-dear to me promises to stay to the end

Ω

I remember the old of the village. I remember the old women: hidden in their sombre scarves of self-accusation, their heart pierced and their abdomen punctured by the spike of an unforgettable and innocent first spasm. Now they are afraid of their ancient lovers and only hope that the altar boys will never know their early virginal secret: that every priest is a man bitterly staring at their wombs. Absentmindedly they idle in their bedrooms now transformed into crematoria of love. Forever nailed by a trembling memory on their weak backs they are slowly lifted onto the crucifix erected over the headboards of their deceased husbands. They are withered into the senselessness of torn cobwebs, along whose threads glide small balls of tears exploding in the trenches of their cheekbones. Those streaming explosives punish the snake-nests of their desires in the vanishing roundness of their breasts.

I remember the old men: they walk with the complaining gait of refugees from the Babylonian exile of vanity and fear. They use their carved canes as a third leg and toothlessly whisper about the suffering of infants nailed to the door-frames of foreign bedrooms. A soft and fragrant cloud of joy has blown away from their permanently humid pipes. And yet they remember the powerful blows of an axe once splitting the last tree trunk of a forest. Three openings of darkness punctuate their gaping faces: two eyes and a mouth, all coloured by the dried-up blood of disappointments. Of their children they know nothing. Extinguished joys of vanished mornings sink to the centre of a hole-ridden tablecloth, a strip of which will serve to tighten their loose jaws

Ω

Women were probably created to enter the desert of our confused and motherless lives. That distant, dignified foretaste of deep loveliness permeates our never satisfied expectations

Ω

The many yesterdays of my childhood have mercilessly closed the cupboard on my dilapidated toys. By now I am no more haunted by them but I still wish to rummage among those treasures of beauty and joy -- maybe for the last time before the greatest toy-maker will show what He has still in store in the line of wonder and amazement

Ω

We were all born with secret imprints that the soul understands as hope, without which there is only melancholy and gloom

Ω

The awesome question 'Why": how often do I fear that to answer the question would have somehow cost me my life. Every day I realize more that 'why' is only a tacit and private dialogue between my inner self and my presumed death. The final answer is not to know, but to forget that there was a question. In some strange way to resist answering is a reason for living.

I remember that even as a child, I used to hide behind a boulder or a big tree, tempted by that question but afraid of the answer. Now I know with some certainty that to answer that great question will occur only when my silence recognizes itself in the arms of another silence

Ω

The trusting soul of man feels at home in woman's dominion, provided that he rewrite the constitution. The trusting soul of a woman feels at home in man's dominion, provided it is her invention

Ω

Tina (my dog) notices something high up in the air that I never see. At first I thought they were birds, but no birds; then airplanes, but no airplanes; then mosquitos, but no mosquitos. Now I think that they are angels -- and why not, since she never barks at them. She never barks at anything I like and admire

Ω

One cannot extract the answer about the beginning and the end of everything, even from God, who knows. Yet ask the scientist...

Ω

When one is poised to philosophize on the term 'abuse', one can rapidly sober up considering a little stone lying on the path. One can either kick it away, throw it at the birds, at a stray cat, at the insulator-cup of a telephone pole, or grandly ignore it.

Instead of picking it up and seeing its honest, ordinary, smooth body crucified in all the calamities of our earth from the moment it was molten lava to the moment of its freezing into an inert something abused until this day. It won't be necessarily grateful to us, but our consideration would activate some of our brain's neurons thus allowing the stone to be coded in a totally new context of existence. We could, perhaps, smooth its reincarnation. Well, almost...

Ω

A tree doesn't think about love. Human beings do. A tree thinks about its own November, when the leaves shimmer in the bare outline of its crown over which are suspended remote and cold constellations. Human beings think about their

38

own November, when they shiver in the bare outline of their lovelessness over which the suspended constellations are remote; yet they signal an irreversible trust in the cosmic order which includes both our lovelessness and our loving

Ω

Someone unknown stands behind each of us and measures our strength when agitated by misfortune and sorrow. An intrepid shadow stands there spelling our names in case we should falter. Our names are given to us in eternity and thus precious beyond time and space. A name which, if invoked, gives the only real consolation to our existence

Ω

We are all people of history and thus the embalmers of corpses. But eventually we may distrust the possibility of resurrection as an unwanted and uncontrolled population explosion

Ω

When we are very joyous and we laugh, there comes a point when suddenly tears appear; laughing exhausts itself in crying. Or better, at the end of joyful abandon there begins a movement within each of us -- a movement toward an ecstatic feeling, away from hilarity but of deep happiness, which goes beyond us into the miraculous goodness of being. There, our tears are the happy sign of bliss in which everything disolves --- even our individuality

Ω

Can innocent people really suffer? Let us consider it. Any act of theirs is an act of loving-kindness and, having very little concern for themselves minimizes the chance of being offended, injured and rejected. Similarly innocent people, being genuinely spiritual people, are incapable of willingly hurting anyone. Their enormous good-will spills over every intention, thus making them benign and protected from evil. Any external hostile act will pass through a sieve of scrupulous consideration of the others' point of view, thus, in advance, understanding their bias and cherishing the benefit of the doubt. Lowered suffering expands their capacity for happiness, resulting in a noble ignorance of unhappiness. Innocence is the only positive defence mechanism that prevents sorrow, misery and violence. It is naturally Christ-like and Buddha-like. Innocence is self-sufficient without the inflation of self-importance.

It may follow that innocence is not a characteristic of children but only of mature people. A child is naturally very egocentric, thus constantly exposed to small frustrations and sufferings. A child is ignorant rather than innocent -- ignorant, in terms of being unable as yet to discriminate and make choices. Their ignorance of evil is evident and natural and yet greatly romanticized by adoring adults. The most difficult transformation of our lives is in our maturing from a bewildered and painful childlike ignorance to a benign and happy adult innocence. Thus innocent people are really not childlike but innocently pure in their maturity.

The only pervasive experience of suffering in innocent people is in their empathy for our unhappiness. They selflessly suffer for our immature ignorance of happiness through our separation from people and from God. It gives me great satisfaction to remember two literary figures I still admire for their innocence: Tolstoy's little taylor Platon Karatayev and Dostoevski's Prince Myshkin

Ω

40

Once I had a friend, far away. A friend of my life. That friend has died. Is my love for him diminished? If it is, I was unworthy of his friendship. Love goes beyond good and evil

Ω

If we cut the roots of a tree, even ever so little, the tree won't die but it becomes a tree-dwarf; if we take away from people their sense of space and freedom, even ever so little, they won't die but will become dwarfs

Ω

Awareness is an awakening from the slumber of ordinary, daily, perceptual, intellectual and behavioural life. Awareness leads to an understanding of Reality beyond any ordinary classification and categorization. If we achieve even a simple level of awareness, we are in some essential way reborn; and, if we achieve a high level of awareness we become enlightened

Ω

Consider that the atoms inside us were shaped and cooked inside distant stars. This happens to be the most ancient culinary experiment, where the ingredients, like iron, carbon, nitrogen and oxygen were provided through the courtesy of remote stars. These vital elements all being immigrants from outer space -- who, please, is the real native on this confused planet? Everything elemental came from somewhere else and the distinction between the foreigner and the home crew is cancelled. There is no Foreign Office in the interstellar immensities -- everything is Home, be it iron in our blood, oxygen on Jupiter or love in our hearts

Ω

A natural, spontaneous urge to sing is an expression of awe and celebration and thus one aspect of spirituality. How could Islam ever forbid it! Singing dissolves harsh pretentious seriousness. Seriousness is atonal and obtuse in its presumptiveness. It is a preoccupation with one's public image and a pharizaic pomposity totally opposite to a melodious free-flow. Singing is a grace and a wonder.

Thus, obviously, I do not mean to include here what parades as singing: the brutal screeching of modern crooners who flood our already contaminated atmosphere with an incessant stream of banal expectorations without grace, without taste, but with an ear-destroying amplification of their own emptiness. No, that is not singing, that is only a vocal commentary on our deep dehumanization and cultural triviality

Ω

When the chalice of our life's wine overturns, we harden into a stain on the cosmic altar-cloth only to be laundered to its original purity -- and we enter the potentiality of a promise 'to be' again

Ω

We seem to have something in common with the dinosaurs. One theory has it that dinosaurs were extinguished because the fern that has laxative properties was not available anymore. Thus, the poor dinosaurs died of constipation. Our human constipation is mostly evident on mental and spiritual levels. We think rubbish, we speak rubbish, we eat rubbish, and we enjoy it -- and rubbish being low on laxative qualities causes chronic constipation. Our mental and spiritual extinction may not be far away

Ω

Snow falls until everything is covered without a trace and silence stands before the wall which separates us from the other side of life -- the one we once knew and have forgotten while living life

Ω

The story of Russian grief. An insane bone-chilling wind rides over Leningrad. You are lost in it, you orphans of the steppe buried in the permafrost of your suffering. Open the strange book in which pain is a bloodstain marking every page and read an ordinary story:

He was alone with his God, an old solitary Russian priest in his tiny wooden church. He was alone when the militia men broke in. They didn't come for his benediction. They carried orders to find some non-existant, hidden barrel of lard; to find it even if it wasn't there. They were simple people, in many circumstances even kind people. Thus they must have been somewhat embarrassed to drag the gray-bearded deacon across the dark vestry of his cerkev. They saw him stumble through the four corners with his little helpless steps like a bewildered mine-pony in the depth of the salt-mines of Siberia. They were even sorry for him when his great blue eyes cried innocence. But he slowly became to them a thorn of nuisance that annoyingly grew under the finger-nails of their patience. Some of them even softly lamented for him when suddenly the inhuman Mask of Horror glued its contorted face to the small windowpane. A small wretched heap of cloth couldn't soak in both the rhythmical jet of blood, and the reddening sky, which indifferently witnessed a murder.

Some might say that they murdered him in utter drunkenness. But they did it because their orders were to do it. After all, duty is a question of discipline, and one is tied to the other just as the vicious dog is tied to a chain. Try to forget even this fearful page, you orphans from the vast steppe. Don't wait for the microbes of hate which will slowly destroy you in your already devastated Pushkin's garden.   More than hate, you need the peaceful grace of Russian birches, pensive lakes, and the burning candelabra of flowers irrepressively growing from the countless graves.

It often rains on the unhappy Russian soil. It rains and the dense fog seeps into the cores of huge stones of fear, sorrow, and tragedy. Who of us ever stops wondering: are you Russians really noble giants dreaming a cruel dream which looms from your tortured souls like a destroyed and submerged cathedral -- a dream like a frozen exclamation mark after a broken sentence about human goodness.

Just to know that this dream will reach the morning. Just to know that this dream is a nightmare and that the real morning is preparing a freshly fragrant breakfast for Bezuchov and Aljosha. Just to know how deep the bottom of your suffering is

Ω

I have difficulties with those lovingly detached women who always know my name, although they have forgotten the social security number of my soul

Ω

A flower grows from within and shows itself on the outside. The real flower is the process of the inner growth -- everything else is incidental

Ω

When time, a placid cow, slowly eats our life on the meadow of our existence, we should rejoice at the thought that the pasture stretches into eternity

Ω

The poorly wound-up clock of our heart doesn't necessarily mean dying but a loss of zest for life. Is there any difference?

Ω

The shifting roundness of a sand-dune reminds me of femininity in its never-arrested passing away

Ω

You thought, and rightly so, that life's crucial task is to live happily. And yet most of the time you feel lonely and fearful that you will remain so forever. You feel lonely, and thus exposed to the merciless glare of the sun that stands at your precise zenith. As long as you feel lonely, you resemble a river that flows for thousands of miles before meeting a village on its shore. But above all,you took a vacation from God, stopped feeling him, and decided instead to do some experimental drilling for the rich crude oil of happiness in temporary distractions. You became a mosquito buzzing a melancholy half-sound; the sound which precedes every song about happiness invented only by reason.

And yet your most important life-task is to live happily. Who, then, prevents you from realizing it? The uncanny propaganda of your incurable ego. It leads you to believe that suffering, with all its potential absurdity, is a vital and necessary condition for happiness. It urges you to accept the tragic sense of life as the most important condition of our existence. And yet tragedy never occurs anywhere in the universe. It is only a human interpretation of the frustrated desires of the ego -- even the nobler ones. Through this basic fallacy we are forced to live a spurious and unnecessary existence of grief and sorrow. And yet your most important life-task is to live happily -- in spite of your jealous and never satisfied ego. What a task!

Ω

45

We read that quartz and onyx are 'semi-precious' stones. Isn't there a possibility that they may resent our declassification? What right do we have? Are we the only precious ones?

Ω

A new olympic event: to push the weight of gravity onto the side of pure goodness. I guess my grandfather would have been among the finalists

Ω

Two occasions When God surely smiles: a) when He notices with amusement that a stick immersed in water brakes into an angle while unbroken; b) when a puppy chews to shreds the golden sandal of an angel. The Great One is always on the side of modern physics, and of abandoned dogs and puppies

Ω

'Adveniat Regnum Tuum' -- ' Let Thy Kingdom Come'. How I like the noble ring of this Latin sentence. Yet, how I disagree with its meaning! I have no doubt that His Kingdom, in its universal form, is always already here; there is no need and necessity to wait for it like for a bus ticket in a queue. We are masochistic in this self-inflicted deprivation of ours. And our various churches support that morbid longing in us.
We are not waiting for Godot. We are sleep-walking unaware that we are holding onto His hand already

Ω

Just a little bit of math; one of the most elegant formulas and yet one with deeply spiritual significance is: the square root of 1=1. Notice, please, that the exponent or variable is equivalent to the constant. A perfect assertion that any fractionality ends in One. The Hindu call it Tat Twam Asi -- You Are It

Ω

How little we care about the mysterious axes that seem to connect the core-structure of all being: the unbroken axis of the atomic nucleus with its neutron; the axis between the sea and the clouds; between tears and happiness; between yesterday and eternity; between what has been, never has been, and is; between our saddened heart and God's

Ω

Whenever we succeed in objectively framing reality and putting it into a statistical coffin, we proudly call our neighbours over to show them our clever achievements. Their sour and reluctant acknowledgement is music to our ears. In our elation we are even willing to lend them our newly acquired lawn-mover. We are so cutely in love with ourselves that we rush to contribute to the United Appeal and resent it only later

Ω

The simple things around us are still calling for our attention, while the wind and the grass run from us in a wave, carrying a whiff of mystery at a never-returning pace. Who ever noticed all the fallen October leaves that are now running away in the company of our most cherished hopes and expectations? If we were attentive to them we would have remembered the sound of a plainsong of no-return; no return even for the simplest things

Ω

Here and there someone is about to grasp the elusive, and we naturally think him insane or arrogant; yet in our best moments we envy him more than the sane

Ω

Back home I had a small old book. A book about robbers and knights. But by now, too many events have flooded the fields between the sweet past and my graying hair. There used to be somewhere, a well, a fence and a gate. To them I attach a drawing of my mother as she is biting into some fruit with such seriousness, as if afraid that in its juice she will fathom all the sorrows creeping past that skinny me whom she endowed with a pathetic glory. Little me before any decision of destiny and thus abandoned to her mercy and love. Little me attached to her as much as to future hurts and heartaches, which she couldn't share as much as she prayed to God to allow it.

She committed herself so irrevocably to this little one that she attached to him all the meaning of the future universe; a universe that would become senseless without the little one in it. So she ate her own time; at the end wasted away through a repetition of unfulfillable prayers for the salvation of all the sons of mothers, one of which is hers. At last she swallowed the merciless fish-bone of her own pain, and at the end, alone, was unable to take in even her beloved and now attenuated God.

And yet the arrow always trembles, a long time after its arrival, and it reverberates in the subdued sound of a silent, uninterrupted dialogue

Ω

My friend has pointed out to me a suitable epitaph to all unfulfilled loves. It is from the end of King Lear:

Kent: I have a journey, Sir, shortly to go; My master calls me, I must not say no.

Albany: The weight of this sad time we must obey; speak what we feel, not what we ought to say

Ω

How precarious is our knowledge. Consider: how little we know of the inside silk of a felt hat; of the last and almost always wasted inch of a string; of the unfinished and cooling oatmeal; of the echo in an abandoned cave; of the rejected stone on the construction site; of the rose petal meeting for the first time a raindrop. How little we know and yet how insanely proud we are even of that little we know. The amazing intricacy of our innermost fathoming goes wasted in the regimented pursuit of the knoweable. We are wastrels of our inborn intelligence and the cringing lackeys of our intellects

Ω

One can solve the problem of a window by throwing a stone through it; one can solve the problem of ice cream by melting it. But one cannot solve the problem of life by death. Neither life nor death are problems -- they are overlapping and interlocked states of being which have no solutions to wait for, since they are absolute certainties

Ω

Do you know what googol is? Just try. A Russian

49

novelist?   A pseudonym of the Archangel Gabriel?   A left-winger for the Bruins? Jaroslav's teasing mood?   No,no, a googol is number 1 followed by 100 zeros, and it is larger than the number of elementary particles in the known universe out to a distance of a few billion light years.   Do I boast about it?   That may be, but mostly I enjoy the notion that even a googol is hopelessly remote from infinity.   While you and I are not

Ω

Not for a second are we ashamed of our orderly filing of reality that falls under the label of successful living.   We are proud that our heap of trivia piles up like useless furniture.   We engage in the ancient human ritual of transporting crates of stale air from one corner to the other; and we charge a handsome fee for that

Ω

Richard Feynman has a splendid phrase: 'Today's brains are yesterday's mashed potatoes'.   Here actually begins the amazing hierarchy of forms and transformations.   We eat mashed potatoes in order to be capable of building cathedrals -- not to become more potatoes ourselves.   We are eating, assimilating, consuming and transforming materials to feed the generator of potentially the loftiest forms of reality.   Forms of reality that our brain proposes after being fuelled and sustained by elementary building blocks.   In some way we are awestruck by God a provider of our bodies and our brains.   Somewhat frightening, isn't it?   Yet it has its poetry.   Yearning for eternity is our greatest appetite.   When we attain it we reach the still point of metaphysical satiation.   The potatoes have completed their mission.
May I add, Dr. Feynman: Today's brains are yesterday's mashed potatoes, and tomorrow's self-actualization and spirituality

Ω

A dilemma of ordinary science: all things can be understood only as an integral wholeness. At the moment when broken and split for examination, the fragments fall into the dust-bin of precarious uncertainty that is essentially untrue to its nature. Scientists should know that any fragmented variable begs a question and the constant doesn't oblige

Ω

We cooperate with others and that implies that we are socially involved in a most necessary and useful function: that of watching others with a suspicion that they might be carrying under their fingernails some undeserved material gains. After all, we are the notorious and self-righteous protectors of justice, especially that justice that favours us. After being overnurtured by the stale diet of self-interest, we sometimes start to experience the nauseating, lukewarm oatmeal of indifference

Ω

An attempted metaphysics of boredom: we are bored to tears by idly eating the pasta of our insipid social co-existence. We are bored as soon as we learn the simple trick of the Skinnerian principle of reinforcement. This continuous haberdashery of unprincipled principles begets an awesome Valhalla of plebeian dehumanization where inanity meets mischievous hypocricy and dullness.

Boredom doesn't die, but keeps on flickering lifelessly. One cannot even use it as the energy to turn from one side to the other. Boredom is the dirt under the fingernails of our souls which has accumulated because we abdicated our intelligence and became ashamed of any contemplation of mystery. More often than not we are indolent troglodytes who are slowly digesting the moratorium of our amazingly dull living

Ω

51

In the approaching dusk we may not be sure how much more we need to acquire, since nothing is allowed on the ferry carrying us across the river of life to the other shore -- just our hearts as life-jackets around the necks of our trusting souls

Ω

How often do we insist that the truth can be folded and put in a wallet? How often do we argue that beauty can be tamed and clipped just like the spoiled poodle of a Hollywood star?

Ω

From the beginning of creation life asks to be heard, not only seen. From the time we are born we concentrate on sounds which adorn like silvery bells the Christmas tree of our inner life. And yet, beyond every conceiveable sound scattered through the vast tent of the audible, far beyond the horizon of our senses, there resounds the universe of the inaudible.

Or is it, perhaps, something truly audible which looms immensely and is constantly transient and receding never to return, once we miss it. Something which even if captured in the net of our imagination would be so remote that we would hear it only long after our deaths. That is the dominion of Amadeus and Johann Sebastian, the weavers of a fathomed-sound reality who in some strange way can help us to capture the inaudible original sound in translation. In essence they offer the 'sound' of imagined silence

Ω

There I stood shortly before dawn, surrounded by the silverware of a starry breakfast and not knowing where to put the last shiny spoon of the cosmic set. And I didn't want to know who I was. I didn't want to know before the morning mass, during which my kneeling is prompted not by my humbleness or my belief, but by my self-defence, since I am at once my own trial judge,my own attorney, my bailiff, and my own grave-digger

Ω

Are we, perhaps, just little round stones being pressed into the mud of the forest road by the hoof of a pensive cosmic cow? Who are we and what were we promised, since we are not allowed to put our hand on the sun, and not allowed to step on the slippery field between an immobile nucleus and an amazingly fast-moving proton? Who are we, who although so distant from an understanding of the real, nevertheless are drawn to search for it in an electron microscope? We only know that when the ordinary morning comes, after a night of laborious investigation, we report in a prestigious journal that the tiny capillaries which surround our nerve endings are the kinky hairdo of our souls. Who is there, then, bursting with laughter?

Ω

When you hurt, a dusk descends onto the forest and recedes to the distant stars. Dusk starts descending while the branches seem to cease to trust in their own enchanted movement. Dust lifts in an ominous cloud of discontent, and your already stooping shoulders resemble more and more the wings of an impaled butterfly in a showcase. That which pretends to be the living tissue of consolation is crushed, like the collapsing scaffolding under which the ashes are deadly pale and bitter tasting. You are still hungry for life, but there is nothing to bite into except your skinny fingers looming like broken arches over a graveyard in which people have buried the golden ring of the promise that goodness endures.

When you hurt there is a procession of days and

nights in which life keeps running by like clear brook water in which you are not allowed to moisten your lips

Ω

Appearances are a hole-riddled reality -- a Swiss cheese through whose holes peeks the serene and eternal 'something' which we can never identify

Ω

It was a lovely morning. Before his routine jogging exercises he had put on brand-new running shoes, and while he was drinking some highly advertized juice from a plastic cup, he suddenly saw through the transparent bottom of it a huge blue eye. For the first time he knew that the answer precedes the question -- and that he is who he is. And he was rather unconcerned, when a para-medic desperately tried to save his life

Ω

What attracts us so hopelessly to our dogs? I dearly wish to know. Surely not their plebeian needs and their fleas. We amusedly recognize that their full belly is, most of the time, their consuming interest. Their running and jumping is a joy to them and a delight to us -- but what more is there? Why are they so mysteriously frightened of 'something'? Why are they so forgiving, so magnificently forgiving, and incapable of malice? Why do they love us without dignity and yet so totally? What is it they like in us, recklessly, without reserve or any second-thought? Where does this religion of theirs originate, since a religion it is in the proper sense of the word? What can we do about their metaphysics of feline hatred? And their liking of fun and play without any inhibition. They may have obtained directly from God a rare licence to be innocent clowns in the circus of living. Why do they like to obey and yet to be mostly bored by it, and to disobey and feel so dejectedly guilty? Why do they detest all the basically benign civil servants around our house: the postmen, the milkmen, the delivery men, the military men, Salvation Army people, and any assortment of band-people? Is it only their guardian instinct or some inborn dislike of anything formal and routinized? They display some of the best characteristics of humanity as well as the worst characteristics of an irresponsible child. Maybe they are some sort of cosmic hybrid, the result of some misguided experiment of creation, half-angels and half-cannibals noisy and slobbering, running out their short lives with such an amazing zest to our deep delight.

There is no doubt, in my mind, that God has an unlicensed dog roaming around Him and, being the greatest Joker of all, He insists that the English language would give to that funny and endearing creature a name which is a simple reversal of His own Holy name, God

Ω

Does God see us in the milky dawn as a propelled spear emerging every day from the night's darkness? Does He mercifully hope for us that the sharp point of that spear will not, on landing, hurt anyone?

Ω

The mosquito of the night buzzes like the mouth-organ of ghosts and cautiously circumnavigates the hot pillow of your concentrated attention, to something that both is and is not. The mosquito doesn't have any intention of waking you up from embroidering your dreams. It merely wants to point out to you that its erratic flight in the dusty cupboard of the night draws a strange arabesque, resembling the outline of your living.

All it wants to point out is that it is as uncertain as you are, as to whether one dreams or is wide awake

Ω

All our life-time we play games as we run helter-skelter on rusting stairs which are rotating upwards like Watson's helix. Until, always rather suddenly, we find ourselves at the end of the ladder and what remains is -- either to jump with a scream, or to step confidently forward

Ω

Sometimes looking at the ceiling, we try to formulate, word by word, some presumably significant pronouncements. But the moment we utter them we are struck by their superficial pomposity and ridiculousness. Then we may wonder, whether the vapour on the window pane is not more real than our pushy and graceless assertiveness

Ω

Let us think of Jewish suffering. Even if you are ready to feel the horror one shouldn't walk on the rails, since with your ears on the cold rail-steel, you might hear a distant death rattle. You will hear the eerie sound of a half-forgotten terror story over which have grown weeds, thistles, dandelions and a terrifying memory that bites into the bones of the sons of man who have sinned against each other so grievously. Even memory has no time to growl; but the usually placid moon snarls and howls when looking over the cancerous growth of the concentration camps.   So that your accusing Jewish mouth might remain silent, they have decided to exterminate you.   Or if that mouth had to exist it must at least be plundered and devastated by the cancer of hatred and violence. Silenced those mouths must be by the butt of a gun, by the heel of a military boot, by a spade, by a needle, by a bullet or by two hands on the throat. As long as they are dead, those gaping mouths are allowed to remain ajar, like unaired rooms in which the fallen angels are warming their unsweetened ration of cruelty on a gas stove.

What do you know, you who have stood on the rusting rails? What do you know about Gehenna-hell that forces you to stop at those rails and freeze to a horror as does a tongue to a frozen iron door-handle behind which they have beaten to death Moishe, Rebecca, Samuel, Aaron, Bashele, Yasha, Isaac...? And what else did they do to you, Jewish people, through the centuries? What did human beings do to you, in front of the indifferent eyes of history long before the gruesome story of the concentration camps? How did they keep silencing you, long before the most recent holocaust?

There is no end of suffering in the history of your pogroms. But since that time there is a new dimension to hell: a mock Requiem of Jewish Extermination sung by the inhabitants of damnation. The sub-title is simple: the Solution for the Unwanted -- the Concentration Camps. There, in the satanic dominion, before death comes, they stretch you on the torture-wheel of hunger. The cruel, shiny boots of the torturers callously step over bodies of the dying to examine scientificaly the unnaturally inflated belly of little Abraham, son of Samuel. Coldly clinical they gloat over the child's excruciating hunger pains. In the morning they find little Abraham, his withered mouth biting through the belt of his dead father Samuel, and his two spent eyes staring in amazed disbelief.

And so they throw his little corpse on the equally disbelieving heap of other corpses, bones, hips, skulls and ribs, there to wait the resurrection. For how many have the mornings passed without the day, for how many the midnights without the dawn? How much of the unending bloodshed has spilled over the horizon of the senseless suffering of those with permanently gaping mouths opened by the soundless shriek of Job's lamentation? And behold the leaden sky overhead, and the never-cooling oven in the quarters of the henchmen of the Curse, who used fractured bones instead of logs to keep warm in the cave of the cold-blooded enormity of their crime. And behold the uncovered craters of earth from which roses had to grow and not the spikes of infamy.

A question of the meaning of the suffering emerges in the Hebraic language and articulates in the Jewish faith, tempted and tested by the clouds of smoke blowing from the slowly cooling chimneys of the crematoria of rejected humanity. Is this the way to be God's chosen people? Only the wise Rabbi knows that human language and thought is vanity in ashes -- while Jehovah watches silently. At last your mouths, you crucified ones, became silent. And that happened when the oven stopped working. Then the rails became rusty, and the whole world began to beat its breast with a cheaply contrite heart and spoke on behalf of the immense crowds of Jewish martyrs.

Why not bring flowers, wreaths, and 'eternal lights' to scatter over the rusting rails? There is a profound reason why not: because flowers are ashamed of us human beings. The 'eternal lights' burn out in a couple of hours, and our formal and pompous wreaths are a plastic reminder of our equally plastic compassion.

If you ever step on those rusting rails, leading to nowhere, you may resemble a sad but faithful God, who is returning to His people over the stubble of their grief, while the lily of the valley endures in its glory

Ω

The origin of our guilt: a state of separation from others. When we feel guilty,we know that we have injured, slighted, rejected, envied another, favouring our own advantage. An abyss looms and we face each other across the precipice with sad resentment. Thus, guilt is actually a sad recognition of our disregard for another -- and we regret it, but not necessarily openly. Here is the point of guilt's frustrating nature. We cannot get free of it without the help of the offended one. We stand separate, torn apart like twins destined to bleed to death in a crude separation. And we enter a vicious circle where we

alternately blame ourselves and the other, resulting in a
continuous open wound of separation. Unfortunately, the
greater the guilty feeling, more resentful of the other we are -- and
the less chance we have to get rid of our guilt and our self-pity

Ω

Surrounded by a mysterious fragrance of
everything that is, I am eating away my day, a sweet-smelling piece
of bread. And am I happy? That I don't know. But grateful yes. I
am deeply grateful that I have received the amazing gift of being
alive. How can I be unhappy? How can I be unhappy if once I was
allowed to bathe with the friendly moon in my country's lake; if
once I was given the privilege of seeing my old dog peacefully
ebb away; if at least once I heard Beethoven's quartet; if once I
was in love

Ω

What else is the greatness of life if not the
awareness of an inexhaustible energy surrounding our personal
time before it merges with radiance of passing time, slowly
merging with eternity. Like a bee becoming encased in ancient,
translucent resin

Ω

We so- called scholars resemble a busy corkscrew
that tries to make a hole through the glass bottom of the bottle of
life -- while its neck is wide open and the splendid wine of
existence freely flows through it

Ω

Our first childhood sadness carries the stigmata of punishment for something as unknown to us as original sin -- and as incomprehensible

Ω

My youth long ago disappeared with a flock of migrant birds behind the horizon. In some deep sense I was allowed to get older because in aging I am more familiar with something enduring, for which I have so strongly longed. Now I am closer to the horizon behind which the birds have disappeared, but I realize that the horizon is not a sharp line dividing this life from a future one -- but is an ever receding phase of reality stretching beyond my time. In getting older, my territory looms larger

Ω

We sometimes imagine that God turns around and whispers: 'Where are you, Joe?' And we, the exemplary altar-boys, will sound a little bell, delighted by His recognition -- and the suffering is over. And who knows whether it may not be as simple as that. This may be the essence of our awakening. The last bead in the rosary of surprises passes over the palm of our hand and we are home

Ω

Look at any tree. It has no objection against its own permanent rootedness. It doesn't want to escape it. Yet its branches carry on a splendid ballet -- a playful game of running away from its own trunk. That is not the gesture of a slave longing for freedom, but of a wise and joyful acceptance of its own destiny -- namely a loyalty to a form and motion given to it by nature. How different we are. Ours is a nervous reluctance to accept any limitations and rootedness. We are mostly so remote from nature

that any gesture of conciliation is primarily felt as a defeat or a
failure

Ω

Notice, that when we smell a rose we are usually
silent. We inhale, absorbing some whiff of immensity without
comment. At once, however, our ego perks up and organizes a
barrage of information. The rare essence of the rose is lost and
the time is spent on learned, encyclopedic, informative clatter. So
any time we discover something subtle, exquisite, it is already
condemned to extinction. For every rare discovery, the bell tolls.
Is it possible that we cannot endure for long any greatness,
subtlety and nobility? Our task is to dissect it, dilute it, break it
down, classify it -- and tastelessly boast about it

Ω

What do you still expect from life? What do you
desire? You may not even want immortality, since surely that is
one of the ego's high-priority desires. You may be surprised to
realize that there is not much more that you want. And since our
life's circumnavigation has already been decided in some cosmic
High Court, what is left is to wait through the passing days; to
confidently wait for the miracle of an ordinary and yet noble life: to
flow like a river into the sea
Ω

The most natural jealousy: a fish seeing a flying
bird disappearing behind the forest. The most natural longing: a
falling leaf remembering that tiny spot on the branch that used to
be its home. The most natural hara-kiri: a rain-cloud impaled by
the needle of a church-steeple

Ω

Most of us experience a longing at a certain time of our lives to leave everything and to kneel down on a dusty road, like St.Paul on his way to Damascus. To kneel down, not to pray, but to be in touch with the earth, our real home, in our most grateful gesture of devotion. Then we become aware that other homes of ours are circumstantial, psychologically motivated and emotionally indispensable -- yet existentially less important: our parents' home, our children's homes, the home of our marriage, the home in our native village, the home of us, prodigal daughters and sons. But only the earth and its supposedly inert matter has elevated us to the mystery of living through some cosmic decision. As Father Zosima reminds us so strongly: we should kiss our Mother of mothers, our earth, often

Ω

Once I fell from my bicycle. Who knows what happened, but suddenly I felt that a cloud of benignity was surrounding me and eyes, numberless eyes, were staring at my little abrasion with such compassion that I forgot the pain. I told my grandfather about it. He took off his bifocals and then I saw his eyes. The same expression which I had already seen before: a compassion so pure and strong that I felt almost at once, and yet in a childlike fashion, that it must be lodged on the other, better side of all things -- and that it melts every sorrow and pain. Yes, the other, better side of things, where I promised myself to spend next year's school-vacation

Ω

I was looking for something in the drawer of my desk. There I found a page from my friend's old letter. Only the second page of it. I wonder what was written on the first, lost page? I don't remember -- and yet, don't I?

Ω

One of my beloved teachers told me that every argument has some blurred, diffused edges; some of those are dark and the others radiate a shimmer. There is no way to understand anything in its depth unless we are guided by the intelligence that fuses this marginal vibration into an instantaneous grasp. Only our intellectual knowing never reveals a resolution of that mysterious blurr

Ω

The image of our death is as empty as a cloudless sky. Any image is based on our memory; and since we don't have any memory of our death, we cannot imagine directly. We can do much better, however. We can start fathoming a timeless and spaceless encounter with energies that surround us, not to destroy, but to invite us to share a never-ending and total cosmic accountability and caring. Our death shouldn't be understood as an Apocalyptic Disaster but as a Magnificent Invitation to dance

Ω

If you are as empty as a flute, you never envy a sack of potatoes

Ω

Recently I have re-read the Psalms. No doubt a literature of great poetry. But in the service of what? Notice some of the content: the prevailing plea is for God's help, for protection, for justice, for help in time of trouble, for victory over enemies, for one's own safety, for rescue from the enemy, for avoiding the company of the worthless, a thanksgiving for saving, for punishing the wicked, for rescue from evil testimony for condemning the wickedness of me, prayer against the enemy etc.

The prevailing atmosphere of self-interest is overwhelming. A maturer compassion is not given consideration. Thus again the question arises: who benefits from the imploring? An unrestrained egotism that begs and whimpers for an improved status and personal self-assertiveness. I came to an alarming conclusion that the Psalms, with all their precious poetry, and some deep wisdom, are not a sacred literature but a lamenting philippic against the 'others' who are hated and despised because they are different. In that sense the Psalms are not a literature of faith but of alienation, self-righteous blame and condemnation

Ω

A fly is buzzing on the window pane; it probably wants to go out. I release it and the crazy creature starts buzzing on the outside wanting to come in

Ω

A man reads in the newspaper about something disastrous. A woman sits, her hands in her lap, and tries hard to listen to him. A bird has flown through the large crown of a tree, and she is awaiting its reappearance. Something in her heart has swayed to one side, and then turned back. Then, just silence. "Tomorrow I must paint that bird-cage"

Ω

During the last war, my uncle, my mother's brother, used to work in an ammunition factory. So did I. We were both forced by the Germans to work there. I was doing some senseless paper-work and he , unlucky as always, was cleaning the sewer. He was ashamed of that work, and my mother often cried because of it. Most of his life he was unemployed, was very poor and had the remarkable face of a cherub. One day I came to visit him, primarily because of my mother. There we stood facing each other across a foul-smelling pool. He was somewhat sadly apologetic, and I was studiously cheerful, and unsure of myself. I remember vividly that not far away from us, on a small marshy island, stood a heron on one leg. I blurted out encouragingly: 'I have some plums in the paper bag, do you want any?' Suddenly I knew that time had stopped; his large, blue eyes became slightly larger and he waved his hand in some timeless gesture of reconciliation with life, with me, with the sewer, and with the solitary heron

Ω

An evening after a tiresome day, and yet an evening of serene awareness. I have opened the window onto a silently falling snow. From somewhere comes a reminder of death. But one without fear -- soft and sisterly

Ω

I was concentrating on my reading and missed the T.V. news. For a second I experienced an annoying twitch but then something within me smiled broadly, lightheartedly and reassuringly

Ω

Some days when I wake up in the morning, I feel that I have only two possibilities: either to worry, or to be cheerful that I am. And just because I have these two possibilities I sometimes feel as light as a white cloud over a mountain peak

Ω

65

It is written somewhere in the Talmud that when you face your God, he will not ask you how much you sinned, but how many opportunities to be happy you wasted

Ω

When during a night's sleep you turn on your side from the room to the wall, you are avoiding something. When after a while you turn from the wall to the room, again you are avoiding something. Only the dead lie on their backs

Ω

There are moments when a person passes us not leaving even a trace in the room or in our memory. Nobody misses him when he leaves, and nobody expects him to arrive. He has disappeared into the crowd, like temptation during confession, and there is not even a hole left after his passing through our indifference. That is the time when God weeps

Ω

Where is the unique consolation that flows from the poet's words? It is in the challenge to all things and all happenings of this life: to wisely refuse the presumed simplicity in everything; to refuse the illusion that life is explicable and subject to a final classification. Poetry is a revolt against the heavy-handedness of our conceited intellect. And so is poetry's sister, spirituality

Ω

When you call your own name, you have the strange feeling that one of you is calling, and the other is assuming that he is being called

Ω

When life becomes extinguished on this planet, there will still be a cosmic consciousness but nobody to perceive anything. Nobody to know time. Nobody to wrestle the angels of anguish, sadness and love. The sorrows and joys of existence will cease. Only the emaciated fingers of rain will tap the veins of the inert substances that always remain ready to be. There won't be a nothingness but an abolished existence receding to meaninglessness, but everlastingly available. Creation may not be happening but still will be intended. It will be a skipped heartbeat of the universal will 'to be', stemming from the sacredness of a creative rest. There won't be faith but a loyalty to the next heartbeat

Ω

The architecture of our soul has become a neglected art for which there is not enough governmental or private support. The interest rate is unsteady, inflation is suspected, and the market value has hit bottom. The stock exchange of our humanity experiences a collapse. The sooner we evaporate as a soulless society, the better the chances for the future renaissance

Ω

We never know what is really too late in our life. But we can form a metaphor that can intimate it: our best joys may be now camping on the other side of the valley, from which we will never come back. Yet it will keep echoing the great beauty and miracle of our existence, through an ever receding but never-ending wave of enchantment, like a chorale composed in our life time but sung for eternity

Ω

To fathom the mystery that surrounds us is like trying to detect the fragrance of a rose from its roots

Ω

Our ordinary life can be so shabby that we attach it as a stamp to a tax return envelope, and mail it to get rid of it, to forget it as soon as possible. Shabbiness in life is the result of our clinging to its tired and un-free one-sidedness

Ω

Joyfulness is an accelerated gallop of the riders of the Apocalypse, who eagerly await the change of the tired horses at the inn of blessing and goodness. Yet, there is never enough joyfulness in our human condition to overcome the darkness, as there is not enough daylight to overcome the cosmic night

Ω

Where there has been recent grief, darkness and longing -- there is now the amazement that all you knew, loved and missed, is slowly filling the cave of your forgetting. What remains is your loving-kindness that endures far beyond those particulars, as an unforgettable witness to its permanent glory

Ω

On a dying man I loved: He is flooded by a sickness, while a shadow of something furtive walks by downcast flowers. How much he wanted to be, and how truthfully. Surrounded by a busy crowd of curious spectators at his last trial, he is detachedly calm. Interested but unafraid, he examines the pale circles around his mouth and notices that his enlarged pupils try to absorb some enormous piece of furniture into his widening visual field. He shivers, sunk in the lukewarm mud of fever, and any time he turns onto his side, there he presses a bony angel under his aching body.

The world has undressed him, and someone else is dressing him up again; and the humming in his ears is the sound of his blood being pushed upstream like the tree-sap in the wrong season. And there is another sound: dry and crisp, as pieces of corn dropped onto the tight drum of his pain. Since his childhood he has walked straight toward his God, yet with a certain impatience.

As he sinks into the darkening well of the evening, as though into the collapsed first floor of a burned down sky-scraper , he knows that the shadow of the bat's wings is trembling on his tired eye-lids. His once beautiful eyes turn up and up in a movement of total purity as he enters the antechamber of an immaculate longing. He is the waiter for Him whom he trusts. And in the moment of exhaustion he listens to the Great Night Music, and that is a moment of fleeting tender bliss. His sickness pecks at him like an absentminded woodpecker on a construction crane; and when it rains he sweats in order not to contradict nature. He is a vulnerable nutshell concerned about its own nut but unafraid of anything, not even of the nutcracker; he is a nutshell on which someone knocks in late afternoon, and keeps knocking.

The hospital visitors come with little golden words on a tight leash, and with uneasy staring eyes that are afraid for themselves. It is up to him to tell them in sublime gestures, that they, as much as he, are soaked in death -- and that actually, one primarily dies from misunderstanding of life. There are so many empty chairs around him and yet there is nowhere to sit down; there is nobody around him to listen to his tacit explanation of something extraordinarily amazing, so clearly known to him. There is nobody around him to join in a play, which though seemingly sad, is totally lighthearted. Mainly he knows, however, that he is elegantly gliding over a dance floor in an accelerated waltz past so many kindly disposed dead people who are soon going to be his hosts. Now the hour of leaving is upon him. His serenity is an amazing, cascading fountain in the middle of life's square, never to be interrupted again.

When I look back at him, he is there no more, but neither is his death

Ω

We do not fully understand ourselves either in joy or in sorrow. We only lean on our own soul and leave on it the finger-prints of longing

Ω

Notice with wonder: what the wise person expresses most truly once in a thousand years, the wind proposes daily whenever it blows through the fluff of a dandelion, dances around the stiffness of ordinary weeds, and twitters in every bird's song. What do we think we really are?

Ω

Something has stealthily evaporated, like smoke leaving the chimney during a dark night. Maybe our life? Something meanders like an arabesque of a groping plant around the rusting spikes of a broken wheel . Maybe our life?

Ω

Caring can be very practical: somebody will lift the collar of your overcoat, will wrap you in your aunt's shawl and will pour a few drops of a good cognac in your afternoon tea. What a feeling of well-being! Caring can be subtle: Somebody will accompany your bewildered eyes on a search for forgiveness, kindly introduce your shadow to its own body, wait for the moment of your amazement and then silently leave. What a feeling of bliss!

Ω

Will you have the same name when you die: Will you be the same? Yes, the same. Exactly the same as the sun, the wind, the stars, the grass -- you will have the same name which you had before being born and which you will have again after you die

Ω

To age is not to grow dimmer and to weakly grope, but to grow telescopically into a vision, as a sonata grows into a finale I feel that such a finale gracioso is the burning of larger and larger holes in the fabric of night until the light prevails

Ω

Revolutions have started because of the human desire to be happy; they invariably fail because of somebody else's desire for another sort of happiness

Ω

71

Our poor tongue never knows which word remains stuck in the network of our over-worked neurons, and which word will join our shy and appreciative soul

Ω

An approaching death could mean a new recognition of things that you never fully noticed before now. And then suddenly, without warning, the cosmic philharmonic orchestra will strike and a fabulous dance will begin -- of everything with everything else: of things with their names, of sounds with the feelings, of bodies with their shadows, of atoms with the supernovas; You never knew before that this ballet can be so hilariously joyful, although performed on the sharp edge of death's razor. You never knew before that Mozart is the brand name of a spread the angels use daily for their breakfast. You never knew before that here one walks on one's head mainly to see the cathedrals from the strange angle of eternity. You never knew before that love is never lost here but leads a welcoming committee on your behalf and assures a paid holiday for all the civil servants from the archangels to ordinary ghosts and goblins. In brief, you are more welcome than you ever knew -- and in case you are wondering about a cloud of bees approaching you rapidly, stay calm, they only house their honey in the most secret cell of your heart

Ω

Although I have received an invitation to some of the lower heavens I keep worrying that somebody is going to deprive me of my promised security. Meanwhile I sanitarily gargle on the antiseptic water of small daily joys hoping to enter the lofty heaven without an embarrassing breath. Otherwise I am a living, resurrected Macbeth worrying about my murderous brand of happiness, while Lady Macbeth fusses about a proper detergent for her guilty hands, thus making our happiness mutually

72

precarious, and as in some marriages virtually impossible

Ω

So little else matters when you are in love, since now you will be sleeping over on the window-sill of your lover's room, now in the windy corner of a bus station. Now you are blissfully nameless while your beloved holds an absurd billboard with your funny name on it. Now you invent silly jokes in order not to explode from interior combustion. Now you arrive on the other side of Jupiter while your lover checks your orbital time in order to send a fleeting kiss as you pass by ...So little matters since everything is as good, trustworthy and beautiful as it was the first morning after the Big Bang

Ω

Vanitas vanitatis: although the angels and their sweethearts will keep gilding the vanishing letters of our names, still their carved edges in the marble slab of our tomb-stone grow shallower and shallower

Ω

Real aging is a more and more frequently repeated proclamation of gratitude, which through its humble grace prepares our understanding of the incomprehensible. The once dense gardens of our turmoil grows sparse; not as the thining hair on the top of our head, but as the progressive unveiling of something essential, as yet only vaguely fathomed.
Naturally, there are the pains punctuating the uncertain harvest. The failing of sight and of hearing, a mist around the high noon of expectations, a torn and bleeding echo of vanished joys, and for the unfortunate ones, the fearful sound

of a shrill trumpet blowing a horrifying sonority of presumed damnation. Yet for some there is at last the serenity, the immaculate conceptions of everything gloriously ripening, the slightly melancholy thanksgiving that cascades over the past -- all in an unrepeatable accent of an oration in praise of life

Ω

God has a funny walking habit: after passing us by -- He begins to return

Ω

Often enough I feel like a boy on a festive day on the gravel path of a park. The crisp sound of the crushed little stones whisper about the passing tribulations that burned the barefoot sole of my lost innocence. Yet, now is the time to gather some wild fowers and to think of aging, while the blue mountains gently recede beyond the sea of hissing, dry grass. There also is somewhere the sound of a gurgling fountain which softly talks of eternity in the brackets of everyday's late afternoon; there is inevitably some tiny inside bleeding, and a longing to go home

Ω

Even the silent and simple things are earth-shaking in their significance. They are the explosive charge of grace that aims to destroy the shaky bridge of my trivial securities and e miscreated artifacts of my desiring

Ω

'Even this will pass'. And what of human love,will it pass and not be? It may, as all the original energies which keep transforming, passing unrepeated, ever new, yet never failing to return to their own source. Love too will pass, but not in the sense of waning, but of differently fulfilling the task of being a blessing to our lives, beyond our understanding

Ω

There are splendid mornings when everything is open like the high windows of a chateau. Everything seems so deceptively simple. Some high, isolated clouds float on their backs and drop white ashes of mist in the ashtray of the valley. The early women air the sleeping quarters and the bold Reverend cleans his morning pipe with a rusty wire from the armour-shirt of a knight-martyr.

And there are mornings when everything is cryptic and suspicious. Where, in the storehouses of forgotten and dusty furniture, something uncanny looms in the fissure between the rotting floor and a musty underground. The freeing wind doesn't enter such mornings, only the shadow of doubts linger there.

And there are mornings of graves slowly entering the immense curve outside of our time and space

Ω

We are inseparable from the centre of everything, and yet since we are individuals, we are unrepeatable, unique. We are indeed, an indispensable ingredient in the bitter-sweet juice of creation, even if so minute that we find a comfortable life-space on the sharp needle-tip of personally alloted time. In the context of cosmic things we are pitifully tiny, and yet there is a greatness to each of us: we are capable of reflecting, and thus in Pascal's sense, we are undistinguishable from universal consciousness

Ω

Orpheus sings only when Euridice is dead.   Is there any other way to celebrate a vanished love?

Ω

Let us see the pattern of human despair and gloom. How often do we sadly think that for us there is mostly only condemnation and nothing else. We pull the blanket of disappointment over our bloodshot eyes, keep winking in self-pity and count the sheep jumping over the fence that separates us from darkness.   Our lament is elongated by the echo of a clumsy prayer and in our intestines rumble our undigested life. We fear that someone unknown is gossiping about us in the borrowed garments of judges.
Yet how wrong we are. We are not being judged, but considered with the most delicate concern for return to our final preservation -- first as a unit and later as a wholeness.   In some inexplicable way, we are celebrated as the most deserving prodigal daughters and sons. We are expected at a home-coming from our birth -- and He who waits for us is the amazingly loving Abba

Ω

I feel as you often do -- like Job peeling off his dried boils, like a hanged man somewhat amused by the sudden abolishment of gravity, like a dead man's shadow which is

exempted from joining him in the casket, like a broken rusty
nail,one half of which will never join the other half

Ω

Once I saw a donkey standing in the street
meditating about the next blow of his master's whip, and the
bellows of his skinny belly were inflated with the hope of some
compassion. At that moment I knew that sadness visits us without
warning and mercilessly, while hope visits timidly and by invitation

Ω

Who is standing behind our back that we fear to
turn around and recognize something we know is there and yet
wish it weren't? This is the metaphysics of horror

Ω

'Is there still something else to know?' the king
asked turning to his clown. 'Yes, Sir. That we love God even in
our insanity'. The king smiled gently and gave him a peach to peel

Ω

I still would like to know how it feels to be a twin of
my left hand, to feel the excited embarrassement of a shucked
corn, to feel the melancholy of a drying pool of water, to feel the
amazement of a little stone kicked away from its humble place after
two centuries of relative uneventfulness, and to feel the joy of a
ribbon found by a girl in the grass behind the church.

Who knows, I may yet feel these things -- after having forgotten so many less important things

Ω

Most mental patients cause a deep uneasiness in psychotherapists. Every troubled mind's chief yearning is: 'Enter into my soul, and don't be afraid of my fears'. Perhaps a spiritual master can do it, but surely not a psychotherapist. He is trained to be an adjustment-agent and not a transforming one. He cannot enter into our souls because he is afraid of our, and his own, ego. He aims at improving our diplomatic relations with the outer world but he cannot induce enlightened changes in our inner world. In order to do so, he would have to be a spiritually committed person. But how many of them are?

Ω

Against all the warnings of our destiny, we turn to look back on our lives like Lot's unfortunate wife, and freeze into a salt-column of self-accusation

Ω

When a bird puts his head under his wing, he is probably sick but not despairing. He may die but he never sins against life. Only we human beings do despair, blaming life and thus sinning against it. Yet life never plots against us, but only allows us to plot against ourselves

Ω

There are letters which we read and put aside, read and burn, read and never remember. Then there are letters never written to us, and those can hurt the most

Ω

There is still so much earth to turn up before we unearth real life. Yet the strategy of life is rather simple: at the end of digging a long mine-shaft, there is light

Ω

Sometimes our soul sings with the abandon of a bird before dusk, totally oblivious to our ego's sorrows

Ω

On the reverse side of every bounced check, an unknown hand writes how much less we owe than what we feared

Ω

Can poetry be courageous? I do not mean this in a political sense, Pasternak, for example. But in the sense of defending every reality by allowing the poetry to penetrate to the mysterious roots of origins, thus dissolving the fear of the unknown. Poetry is written by people who know that they are like an apple tree that knows that its own waning flower is the intimation of an apple, and the apple is an intimation of an apple seed, where the circle begins and where,presumably, it returns. The poet knows that all that is presumably known must be courageously assured of its endless return, thus allowing the removal of any boundaries to the miracle of reality. The poet's

79

courage is a bold confrontation with the unknown from which
other people shrink with anxiety

Ω

When Brutus was shaving before the battle of
Filipi, he feared two deaths: Ceasar's and his own. We fear only
one death, and yet when shaving in the morning, we dread the
other eyes that belong more to the back of the mirror than to us

Ω

There it stood beside the ditch, humble, shy,
dusty, dishevelled, crooked and unnoticed. An ordinary weed.
While I passed by preoccupied with some useless problem, I
didn't pay any attention to it. I wasted the chance to give it the
grace of recognition

Ω

Essentially you and I are ineffable, but only up to
that moment when both us will be permanently evident but
missing and lost in the cobweb of mystery

Ω

What do we know about eternity when even the
prophets, gurus, masters, and saints couldn't wipe off of their grim
faces the dust of unknowing? What do we know even about the
ordinary things that are strung upon the operating table of our
cold observation, and do not yield the truth but only an
unaesthetic stiffening?

Ω

There is construction work going on within me all the time. Something is removed, something imported, something forgotten, something remembered, something is breaking down. Something flows out of my mouth like the sound of an injured flute. Some huge steel crane lifts me to a standing position. A lot of dust blinds my eyes. I keep talking pidgin English while someone is reading aloud Ezra Pound. And yet the cathedral is far from finished, and as time passes, I only care that its ceiling remains incomplete so that I can safely float through its opening when it is flooded

Ω

I resemble a choking fish on a dry shore. The open mouth wants to say something, the gills are straining and someone's calm eye is examining my throat which is desperately forming a question. A question that doesn't begin in my throat, but at the bottom of the sea

Ω

What will I be when I am not what I was anymore? Here the basic assumption is that I really was. But what if this assumption is spurious? Then the question collapses. And what used to be 'I am' changes into 'am'. That may be the whole trick of my immortality

Ω

The wooden floor sometimes cracks like a frozen lake from the steps of those who left a long time ago, and who now return barefoot through the drying meadows of our memory.

And as everything, they were once, are no more and yet loom as high as an Egyptian obelisk surrounded by a lace of restless shadow. We miss all of those who have passed away -- and we miss them again when they return

Ω

Even in an unborn infant there may be a germ of longing to remove a stone from the tomb of God. There, somewhere, is the beginning of human nostalgia

Ω

Abraham was invited to sacrifice his beloved son Isaac, the most precious flower of his life. To be in faith is to be invited to this sacrifice, the deepest challenge for trusting love. If understood, the curtain of faith begins to reveal eternity.
God didn't deprive Abraham of his dearest son, as God never intends to, but tried his faith in Him. If there is an instance of the deep silence of benediction, it is the silence of Abraham's trusting heart contemplating God's face, while the fear for Isaac dissipates like a mist heated by the rays of the sun

Ω

In autumn, birds congregate in a magnificent show of cosmic memory: to follow the intimation of an eternal return

Ω

Have you ever seen a butterfly dying? If so, you have seen the swerving of a lofty conciliation before it sinks into the heart of silence. It is the merry twitter of a burning candle in the glow of an autumnal afternoon. You have seen an ancient thanksgiving for death that doesn't interfere and doesn't disturb.

That gentle slowed trembling of a butterfly becomes a mysterious flow of energy that, without gravity, sinks between our amazement and the passing away of everything. The butterfly doesn't crumble out of fear of dying, but becomes a blissful messenger of transition in a sublime dance with a beam of light that returns to the source of the universe. The butterfly doesn't die but falls away like the flower of a cherry tree, awaiting its transformation to a cherryfruit, which in time, becomes a flower again.

Like our soul, the butterfly hopes to return to the twilight of Mothers, who sit in endless rows around the high fire of creation patiently waiting for the sun-rise return of their children through the portal of death. It dies in a blissful swerving, in an ecstasy of obedience, surrounded by the incandescent colours of its own wings, just ready to alight finally and motionlessly on a blade of grass

Ω

We search in the clouds for what has evaporated from our lives; but the clouds are torn and shredded vapours. Rarely do we change our point of view by noticing in the background of the clouds, the serene blue sky

Ω

Because we are so preoccupied with ourselves, we keep asking questions. After all, most of our questions are stuffed with fear that we have missed something and we may not

get it in good time. Any question is essentially a subtle
expression of a greed for more that eventually could enhance our
success in the competitive ranking

Ω

Love is always an Agnus Dei: immaculate,
vulnerable, often crucified,as cherished by Him as the pupil of the
eye. A lamb of God, released at the dawn of creation and since
that time grazing in the pastures of life to be attended by mortal
shepherds -- and sadly called back home to the shed of divine
mercy, when unattended

Ω

Often, modern man appears to be a castrate with
a high-pitched voice singing the praises of our sprawling cancer of
concrete, of pneumatic drills, chain-saws, motor boats, oil-pumps,
bulldozers, our garage-sales of sentimentality, of indexed
pension plans. We speak of progress walking on a conveyor-belt
which is running backwards. We are trying to be the pillars of
society, with brutal ambition to be top-dogs. And we impotently
hope that our success is a matter of cosmic significance

Ω

The deepest lovers are taciturn. They draw
circles in the sand, collect in the basket of their amazement the
receding footsteps of a smiling God, and search at the bottom of
the transparent pool of each other's eyes the silver key to open
the private chapel for a festival of radiance, trust, and humble
reverence for any love

Ω

84

Even our own face will pass away, since we must
return to the substance that is One and, thus, a depository and
transformer of all forms. I do not think that eventually we return
after the day of Judgement to the existence of our
glory-surrounded body. The substance and essence of the
universe, being divine, is already our glorification, and in the
instance of transformation there is no special higher, lower, or
neutral status. We become one, and that is our glory. We
wouldn't need glorified bodies as a further 'compensation' or
'reward'. We become part of the implicit order of everything -- and
not an explicit temporary existence, re-emerging in our
recognizable form

Ω

And there is still so much yet to be heard after the
wind has gently moved a weed behind the fence, when the low
clouds have passed a deep forest, when the sun has suddenly
fallen into a puddle and when the night has tied up the moon on
the top of a stately oak tree. There always remains the listening to
the inexpressible something, after someone has said his last word
of gratitude, after the pebble has turned under the hoof of a
wandering reindeer, and after the slow movement of a quartet in
its awesome after-sound. Then we become absorbed in the other
side of reality which we have longed for since birth. We become
absorbed in that magnificent voice singing without a pause to the
living and to the dead

Ω

How alone, really, are we, without being lonely?
Alone as a rusting nail in a broken plank; a stuffed and dusty eagle
in an abandoned lodge; a church organ in the darkness of
midnight; an actor wiping off his make- up after the last act; a
table-cloth after supper; a pain of jealousy during a wedding
ceremony; an elderly person and her cane late on Sunday
afternoon.

All these metaphors are not the stuff of which dreams are made, but symbols of bare reality, yet we must still keep going before someone turns around and notices us desperately trying to keep pace with Him. Then we will be picked up like tired kittens and pressed gently against a warm immensity. No more traveling on our own -- so many, many things to tell about our separation from lovely and strange people, now already so remote on a distant speck of real estate, to which we will probably never return, and never be alone, anymore

Ω

We live through some inner earthquakes which at that moment signal disaster to us, but later prove to be just the peeling of the aging wall-paper of futile and useless worries

Ω

Sometimes, not always, we all feel lonely and abandoned, like a statue in a gallery closed for summer renovations

Ω

At our death, the universe will concentrate for a millisecond on our cooling, small protoplasmic soup, and kindly inform us that we were, after all not planned as anything other than what we are, even from eternity -- an unimaginable possibility. Is that anything to be frightend of?

Ω

I have always missed (maybe due to a wishful imagination) a fragment of a secret film from the concentration camps. Namely, that scene where the condemned victims, led to the brink of a freshly dug common grave, suddenly stop and begin to hit, slash, crash and destroy the inhuman jailors. With their bare hands, broken bones and skulls, with their remaining teeth, or empty, bleeding gums they attack the executioners. Destroy them, if not for any other reason than that fearlessness in the face of death is one of the noblest of human virtues.

The victims do not attack out of a desparate anger or a vicious need for revenge, but to insist in a powerful gesture of persuasion, that nobody can put human beings to death -- only their own utter despair and resignation

Ω

To be a bystander has an advatage: the other, and not you, has been hit. To be a bystander has a disadvantage: society forces you to testify

Ω

As much as I hate whistling, I wish some people would whistle, instead of talking. Their puckered cheeks can be deflated easier than their inflated conceit

Ω

Individuality is a transfer on the bus of being that never stops. We must simply change the ticket from individual existence to universal being, when we die, and from being to individuality, when we are born. Otherwise the ride on the bus is the same, and the country-side is as splendid as Val D'Aosta

Ω

87

You can make a life decision that will result, invariably, in not being taken seriously by society. You can spend the rest of your life observing clouds, butterflies, children, birds and trees. You will gain an incomparable mental freedom, and yet you will be accused of social non-cooperation. It is a natural dilemma of our civilization. Yet to be able to attend to both levels of life's involvement is a sign of real liberation

Ω

The more we insist on dry cleaning our frightened existence, the more bleached will become our character

Ω

Out-of-this-world scenario: When you next see the Benedictine monks of the Jupiter playing soccer against the Martian Trapists, Gozzoli's angels sticking their tongues out at you, St. Jerome registering for the classical marathon, St. Teresa jumping from the high board while John of the Cross changes his swim-trunks in the dense bulrushes not far away, Bach's own choir-boys returning from a musical contest with the Kremlin Politburo Singers, and the Tibetan Buddhists breeding their beloved dogs for profit -- you have bought yourself a ticket for a benefit played for the orphans of eternity at the corner of Fifth Avenue and the Milky Way Place entitled: "Requiem: Much ado about nothing"

Ω

Hamlet's son, if he had ever been born, would have called Ophelia his mother. He would have remembered so many things from his early childhood, especially his stuffed clown,

88

whom he used to feed with a wooden spoon while the palace darkened and its mysterious corners emitted musty coolness. The toy clown was actually made for him by the faithful Yorick, who used to be a tutor to his father. He would both love and detest his early memories. His perspicacious brain would know that he had his father's hot temper and an inclination toward melancholy. From his mother he would inherit a strangely vibrant sensitivity. This would make him conclude that the ever-present and beloved moon sometimes appears far away, sometimes very close, but never in the reach of his hand as are other trustful and confidently tame things. For those truthful and yet evasive things he would pine more than for people. He would be alone when the sound of the blind musician's flute roams around Elsinore's fortifications. This music is as pure as a forest spring left to its own meditation, and like a rose staring at the sun.

He would be mostly precocious, witty to his detriment and as painfully cantankerous as a boil on a nose. He would belong nowhere. His mood would be conspiratorial and mistrusting, like that of a bee alert before the morning unfolding of a violet. While still a teenager, he would ride for endless hours the king's pure-bred horses, thus aggravating the stable-hands who loathed sweaty and overheated animals.

He would often torment his own tutors and sometimes leave droplets of honey between the pages of their wit-befogging tomes. He would have no friends, for friends are for the joy of the soul, and he wouldn't enjoy anything, not even his soul. He wouldn't believe it belonged to him. And since he is Hamlet's son, he would be pervaded by the ever-so-soft bitterness of almonds; but yet, also, by the loyalty of a fruit's stem to its stone. And since he is Hamlet's son, he would write a philosophical testament found after his untimely death under the lining of his hunting jacket:

"When you accidently see God at work, you may detect on his sleeveless arm a tatooed picture of yourself. Then you experience gooseflesh similar to that my father felt when the poison from Laertes' sword entered his bloodstream"

"Who shall say how often it has already rained on a stone"

"On each and every grass-blade falls one droplet of grace"

Ω

When we experience an enlightenment, however imperfect and of short duration, our brain fumes like an overloaded electric circuit. In a split second, our vanity turns into dust, and someone leads us to a cliff where we remain stricken with astonishment that levitation is possible if chosen. It is at such a moment that human beings cease to gyrate around their own axis. The squashed cockroach of any problem remains stuck to the sole of a new understanding full of insight, humour and trustful patience

Ω

'Now' is the most genuine bond of the universal duration with a particular accent on the immediate fragment of experiencing. It is the greening of our time, a luxuriant release of eternally stored colours into a rainbow that appears to all of us, but in a split second of a different time.

'Yesterday' is a huge musty museum of events and inventions that have been fixed forever. It is a collection of dead insects in a glass case, awaiting today's classification and judgement. It is a plastic flower in a transparent container, never to be touched or smelled.

'Tomorrow' is an embalmed mummy of yesterday, loaded on a slow freight train of awaiting, an expired pastness transferred into the future by our intentions and our language. This futuristic cocoon will never be a butterfly, since a butterfly is in existence when the cocoon no longer is

Ω

90

Ω

What the Zen people would call a horizontalizing of the mast of ego stands, not only for the notion of human humility, but for the mastery of mental sailing

Ω

We never renew ourselves more than in our moments of genuine mirth. We become clean again like dusty leaves after a rain. Thus in mirth we return to our source and are suddenly surrounded by a fearless benediction -- the twin of happiness

Ω

Inner silence is a privilege of the few. It is cross-country skiing on the hills of awe, and the only sound is the confident hiss of the skis pointing to the white horizon

Ω

Not even a T.V. anchor-man can change the fact that whatever you are, you never have been a failure -- the senseless gymnastics of a mosquito on the window pane. You have been and you are: that is a superb distinction in itsef

Ω

I have always liked the late afternoon. That is the time when a gentle wind of well-being surrounds me, the way the golden dust of a dandelion meadow surrounds a stray dog passing through it

Ω

I knew him as a young priest. He sat solitary and taciturn in the overcoat of the murky sunset of suburbia that reluctantly narrows into the bottlenecks of empty skyscrapers. He sat lonely in the cross fire of the search-lights of faith and melancholy hope, his forehead in his hands and behind him a darkening slum. His dream was of the city of God. Only the dust, the eye-witness of the wind, was rising from the port-side. He still hoped that resurrection would occur in his city , like grace coming as a spring bud to a candelabra of the sprawling branches of a never-despairing tree. He sat taciturn and the city had the ironical smile of a detached whore

Ω

I always admired the small wayside shrines of our country. They are built, as it were, from the unearthly stones of peasants' devotion. They stand, these minute churches, in the midst of the fields like tiny vases of simple flowers on a table-cloth of undulating wheat. They have a small altar, a diminutive place for kneeling where one has a good chance of inadvertently elbowing an invisible angel. In the distance are the white-washed chimneys of farm houses, and a handful of poplars looming like unhammered nails on the lake- shore.

Each of the countless visitors approaches through the high, fading grass with a heart of joy, or sorrow, or pious contemplation. One came, a long time ago, on horse-back. The rein was loose, the sabre clinked against the stirrup, and there was dust everywhere: on the horse, on the tired rider and on his heart. The dried blood on his forehead could have been his own or somebody else's. The smoke of a burning castle still clung to his leather coat, and kneeling down to the Virgin, he gloomily thought of his brother Christopher who was injured and remained behind.

Another, on a black, torn night, carried a suicidal thought like a heavy oil-oozing sack. And when a glistening needle of lightning darned together two pieces of the night's brocade, the light fell sharply on a pistol and on the Virgin's gentle smile in the niche behind the altar.

Another, a shepherd, softly inclining his head, remained sweetly alone and oblivious to time. He spoke a prayer for all souls with a humble simplicity, like a sparrow sprinkling itself in a small pool of water left behind from the night's rain.

One came, whom bliss took by the hand. Innocent and hopelessly excited by his early love for Magdalena, offered field-flowers to Mary's picture, whispered transparent sentences of ecstasy, and absent-mindedly dusted off the forehead of a plaster statue of the baby Jesus.

Another came, invoking in vain the dearest name in the empty fields. She knelt down on the cold pavement of her abandonment like a lonely star of the Pleiads pining for a star of a distant constellation. Betrayed, cut in half by the cruel sword of an untrue love, she whispered to the Compassionate. But no words, no sighs came, just a horrible rattle of an injured soul incapable of returning to itself. One for whom the journey to the shrine was a painful effort, came on crutches supporting the unfinished arch of her aging. She was indifferent to what makes a difference in a meaningful life. She was not unlike the furrowed bark of a long dead tree donning a carnival mask of a bat's withered face. She was removed from her own roots and feebly whispered in one tired sentence: "Why still...". She was an impacted tooth in the painful confluence of life's little joys and life's many poisons. There she stood, close to the altar, listlessly staring at an aging God, who is always bleeding from His left side.

And there was one, young and pious, who came with priestly dignity and full knowledge of prayers and genuflexions. He was tall and skinny, dangling and eager, and so tender in removing the cobwebs from the consecrated twig of a willow. He was happy in the valley of his peace, and blissfully half-closed his eyes as he recognized a silver cross quivering through the distant sound of the bells.

They have all visited the old wayside shrine, only

vaguely aware of the fragrance of grace that dwells in everything, yet passes by as mysteriously as the flight of a swallow

Ω

Often in the mid-road of our lives, we crack as a bronze bell in a frozen Russian church. And when the crack keeps running through our fundament, we start mistrusting the miracle of transformation and begin to eat the dust with tears

Ω

I know that eternity passess even under my life's ceiling. And I am amazed that it is as close to me as sap is to the stem. That is a time for deep rejoicing, since, for a brief instance, I am allowed to see the opening through which I will be returning home

Ω

There is always some last station on the railway of our little tired, but still enchanted life. Beyond it the rusty rails fade out in a carpet of ever-welcoming flowers. From here we must travel on our own feet, rain or shine, to the narrow opening of the horizon which points to everything we ever trusted. Barefoot and alone

Ω

LONDON PUBLIC LIBRARY
DATE DUE
